GLORIOUS STENCILLING

GLORIOUS STENCILLING

Elaine Green

Colour
Library
Direct

Dedication
For my husband, Ian

A QUINTET BOOK

CLD 21153
This book was first published in 1998 for
Colour Library Direct
Godalming Business Centre
Woolsack Way
Godalming
Surrey GU7 1XW

ISBN 1-85833-948-0

This book was designed and produced by
Quintet Publishing Limited
6 Blundell Street
London N7 9BH

Creative Director: Richard Dewing
Art Director: Silke Braun
Designer: Steve West
Project Editor: Clare Hubbard
Editor: Anna Bennett
Photographer: Jonathan Russell Reed
Illustrator: Jennie Doodge

Typeset in Great Britain by
Central Southern Typesetters, Eastbourne
Manufactured in Singapore by Bright Arts Pte Ltd.
Printed in China by Leefung-Asco Printers Ltd.

Publisher's Note
When completing stencilling projects exercise care when using tools and materials. Always follow the safety instructions given in this book, and always read the manufacturer's instructions on packages and labels. Use paints containing lead with care and when painting surfaces or items for children it is essential to use lead-free, non-toxic paints. If using spray paints, always wear goggles and a protective mask and work in a well-ventilated area. To avoid inhaling the dust when sanding or sawing MDF a protective mask should be worn.

All statements, information, and advice given in this book regarding methods and techniques are believed to be true and accurate. The author, copyright holders, and the publisher cannot accept any legal liability for errors or omissions.

CONTENTS

INTRODUCTION

Stencilling is an immensely popular and enjoyable way of decorating, with unlimited creative potential. Applying a stencil is a technique that can easily be mastered by almost anyone, even those who claim to have no graphic skills at all, using materials that are readily available and relatively inexpensive, so that beginners need not feel daunted. Thanks to the availability of pre-cut stencils in a wide range of interesting designs, professional results can be obtained with minimal effort. For those who prefer to design their own stencils, the possibilities are endless.

Although I have been stencilling for many years, the moment when the stencil is peeled back to reveal the image of a new design for the first time never fails to excite me. During recent years stencilling has moved on from the tentative borders used initially to far more adventurous finishes and effects. Once you have mastered the basic techniques, you can experiment with different finishes and effects: try stencilling using a tinted gloss varnish over a matt base to imitate damask-like patterns, for example, or building up richness by overlaying one stencil over another.

This book aims to teach you the basics by taking you through a variety of projects ranging from simple stencilling onto paper up to planning and decorating a whole room. You will discover some of the exciting ways in which stencils can be used either by making use of the stencils at the back of the book or by designing your own. I have included a number of different paints and techniques which are all quite simple to use and which I hope will lead you to further experiments. I have tried to show how you can achieve exciting results by thoughtful arrangement of the stencils themselves and careful consideration of the background on which they are to be placed. Detailed descriptions are given for each project and some advice on finishes has also been included. The idea is for you to use from the projects described the steps you may wish to select for your own piece of work. The advance planning is half the fun. At each stage of your work you will be making decisions leading towards a completely individual and personal project. It has been a great pleasure to me that Caroline Brown has agreed to contribute three projects showing her lovely textiles together with a detailed description of the technique of spray painting, a method which produces unique and beautiful results. Caroline and I met over 12 years ago while learning our stencilling skills from the master stenciller Lyn Le Grice. We had not met again until now and as we have both been stencilling continuously since then it has been fun catching up and interchanging ideas.

Stencils found on the walls of a fifteenth century English house.

NOTE

In order to complete the projects, trace off the relevant stencil and cut it out before you begin work. Where a press-out stencil has been provided, this will be noted in the relevant project.

An age-old craft

Stencilling has been defined as 'a drawing or printing plate with parts cut out to form a design that is to be copied onto a surface by laying the plate onto the surface and painting over the cut-out parts.' The word itself is derived from the old French *estencillir*, which means to sparkle. Stencilling has been used as a method of decorating for many hundreds of years throughout the world, each country giving to the craft its own national characteristics. In England evidence of its use can be seen in churches dating from mediaeval times when it was frequently used as a background design on the decorated rood screens separating the nave from the choir, or to imitate the designs on rich fabrics worn by painted figures. Ancient stencil designs are still being discovered and preserved today, not only in churches but also in domestic dwellings that retain their original decorations. Sadly, over the years not everyone has recognised this work for what it is and a number of fine examples have been painted over. Today, with a greater interest in stencil decoration, owners of old houses are more likely to recognise early forms of this craft if they come across it and can contact the appropriate experts and have records taken before they start redecorating. Stencilling in England has been used continually as a way of decorating and the work of many famous names of the past such as Pugin, Burges and Charles Rennie Mackintosh are still to be seen in all their colourful glory.

Stencilling is believed to have originated as an art form in China, possibly as early as 3,000 BC. It spread to Japan where some examples of the work were so fine that the bridges linking the designs were made of human hair and virtually invisible. The Japanese also stencilled both sides when working on cloth so that the fabric looked as if it was woven. The countries of continental Europe have their own strong stencilling traditions, some of which found their way to colonial America where settlers used stencils as a way of decorating furniture, floors and floor cloths. Examples have been found dating back to 1778.

You can see many examples of stencilling in museums, on items such as furniture, quilts and rugs, which could be used as a starting point for the creation of your own designs.

As this is first and foremost a practical book, the background I have given is of necessity only a very brief introduction to the rich and varied story of stencilling. I have suggested some books for further reading at the end if you want to learn more. The advantage we have over our ancestors is the great diversity of convenient modern materials designed to make our work easier and quicker. There is greater attention to the safety aspect and as you will see in the following pages many products are now water-based and non-toxic and their quick-drying properties mean that we can avoid unpleasant fumes without compromising the quality of the finished work.

I very much hope you will find something in this book that catches your imagination and gives you the confidence to get started. Have fun!

Wreath of Roses quilt (78 in/
200 cm square), American,
mid-nineteenth century.

American dower chest,
painted in Pennsylvania
Dutch style, c. 1785.

A stencilled floor in the American
Museum, Bath, England.

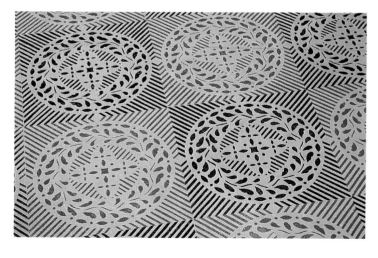

THE BASICS

A major advantage of decorating with stencils is that the tools and materials required need not be expensive. It is a craft where you can gradually build up your equipment as you need it, and if you are prepared to design and cut out your own stencils not only will you have the satisfaction of producing your own designs, but there is a considerable financial saving involved.

Be inventive with 'found' household materials such as kitchen sponges for applying paint, or tying string around a foam roller so that the finished effect is mottled rather than flat. Keep empty yoghurt pots to use as disposable containers for paint and varnish. Clean your brushes by rubbing the bristles across the rough surface of nylon pot cleaners. Save old tights for sieving lumpy paint and use old T-shirts for ragging on paints.

Remember that a simple design placed with imagination can be just as effective as something more complicated and ambitious.

Think about the space created around the stencil shape as much as the shape itself. Spend time trying out your ideas before you start. Having put time and effort into cutting out your stencil, try and get as much out of it as possible – see what it looks like upside down, flip it over to make a mirror image, try repeating it at regular intervals to make a border, and experiment with some of the different techniques described for applying paint. You will find suggestions to help you to organise your work in advance; time and effort spent measuring and working out where to place your design to the best advantage before you start will be well rewarded, even though you are longing to get going.

MATERIALS

Measuring equipment

Pair of compasses for drawing circles on geometric stencil patterns; dressmaker's measuring tape for use when working on fabrics; long metal retractable tape for general measuring and for walls; set square, especially useful when making floor cloths and checking corners; plumb line (a long piece of string with a weight on the end) to check that lines from floor to ceiling are vertical. (An improvised line can be made from a length of string with a key on the bottom; long non-slip metal rule, useful when working out border

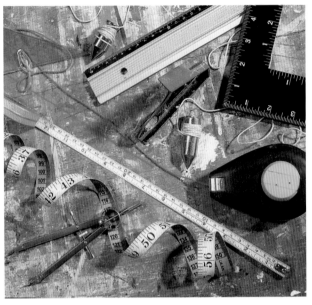

designs, measuring generally (especially floor cloths) and also for cutting straight lines on stencils; small spirit level, to check the level of borders around the top of a room where the ceiling line is uneven; large metal square for squaring off stencil card for large stencils and for checking corners accurately, especially when making floor cloths; chalk box, a box filled with chalk containing a long length of string (its use is described in detail in the floor-decorating project).

Masking tapes and glues

Two-sided tape for securing floor cloths to stop them slipping; 1 cm (½ in); and 2 cm (1 in) masking tape invaluable for stencilling, repairing stencils, masking areas and so on. Do not leave tape on items longer than the manufacturer recommends, as it can be very difficult to remove after a while and could remove the background on which you are working; red sign writer's low tack tape, suitable for marking out lines. Adhesive, solvent-free craft glue used in floor-cloth making; fine line tape, a very fine low tack tape especially helpful for making thin lines on furniture (see the Writing Slope project page 53); stretch tape for marking out curved surfaces; low tack stencil tape; re-positional non-permanent adhesive; paper glue; 6 cm (2½ in) low tack decorator's tape, useful for masking round stencils, marking out stripes on walls and so on. In the centre of the photograph is poster tack, useful for fixing stencils in position on surfaces where non-permanent adhesive would be unsuitable. A tube of border and repair adhesive (not shown) is useful when working on a wallpapered wall where the wallpaper is peeling off.

Stay-wet palette
Made by various artist's paint manufacturers, useful for keeping acrylic paints moist. The paints can be kept for some time once squeezed on to the surface, with the lid in place.

Equipment for applying paint
Marine sponge for creating background texture and for applying paints through the stencil plate; 5 cm (2 in) sponge roller for stencilling larger shapes and for rolling on background paint. A mini roller, an alternative way of passing the paints through the stencil, covers very quickly and can make light work of stencilling large areas of background; you can then fill in the details with a brush. A roller can also have a different colour at each end, which gives the design an interesting mottled look when passed through the stencil; a range of brushes in various sizes for painting in the background to be stencilled. The diagonal fitch is useful for awkward corners and areas where an accurate edge is needed; a commercially produced brush cleaner (the green square shown). Stencil brushes should always be washed out as soon as work is finished (acrylic paint is particularly difficult to remove if left on). Having washed out the brush in warm soapy water, rub it across the brush cleaner to remove any residual paint. An alternative is to rub the tips of the brush across a nylon scourer; the black roller tray is for use with sponge rollers. Put several teaspoons of paint into the well, run the roller across this then even out the paint by running the roller across the ridged top of the tray; in the centre is a range of stencil brushes of different sizes, the large ones for stencils with large coverage such as floors and very small ones for

detailed work. Always buy the very best stencil brushes you can afford. For each new stencilling job you will need a separate brush for each colour group. It is worth taking good care of your brushes and storing them properly (bristles upwards) so that bristles do not become damaged. Always make sure that you have a set of clean and dry brushes for each job.

Papers and stencil card
Cartridge paper for working out design ideas; acetate for making stencils; carbon paper, useful for transferring a design onto stencil cards; (should not be used to transfer a design onto the object to be decorated as the marks are difficult to remove) graphite paper for transferring marks directly onto the object to be decorated; tracing paper for tracing designs; decorator's lining paper, an inexpensive but useful paper for testing out designs, masking out areas and so on; oiled Manila stencil card for making stencils; on top of the Manila card is a second type of acetate for making stencils. A number of different types are available, but the best are those with a rough side on which you can draw; in the centre, graph paper for working out regular and geometric patterns. Not shown, but useful, is overhead projector film suitable for photocopiers (available from office suppliers) – the design can be photocopied directly onto this.

PAINTS

Most paints are suitable for stencilling so long as they dry quickly and are of a creamy consistency so that they will not run under the stencils. There are a number of paints produced especially for stencilling but I prefer the freedom of mixing my own colours and I usually use acrylic tube paints. It is preferable to buy artist's quality colours where possible; not only are the colours better, but they also have a higher degree of permanence.

NOTE It is always important when using new products to read the manufacturers' instructions carefully and to act on their advice for the best results.

Acrylic paints

They are water-soluble, flow well and come in a wide range of colours. As they dry very quickly it can sometimes help to mix in a small amount of acrylic retardant to delay the drying time. Brushes should be washed in warm soapy water immediately after use, as the paint is very difficult to remove if it is allowed to harden on the brush. Liquid acrylic paints are also available, which are dispensed with a dropper and are very convenient to use.

Emulsion or latex

Many decorator's merchants sell sample pots as testers. These are an ideal size for stencil painting. The solvent is water and brushes should be washed out as soon as you have finished. These paints are also very suitable for covering large areas and work well with mini rollers or 5 cm (2 in) rollers for speed.

Spray paints

These paints are particularly suitable for painting onto surfaces such as enamelled fridge doors, glass windows and most other surfaces with the exception of ceramic tiles. The big advantage is that there is no equipment to clean. The use of spray paint is described in detail on pages 24–25. They do require a little practice but, with patience, you will eventually achieve rewarding results. The solvent for these if you are using them on hard surfaces is acetone or a small amount of cellulose thinners. Be careful with the latter as they can remove the background paint as well.

Sign writer's enamels

These paints give a good, luminous coverage. They work well for stencilling onto all surfaces and can be used on glass and stove enamel such as refrigerators. Some produce a translucent effect similar to stained glass. The solvent is white spirit. Because some of these paints contain lead they are not suitable for children's furniture or toys.

Japan paints

These have good colours and are quick-drying but, although very well thought of, they are not available everywhere. The solvent is white spirit.

Oil paints

These can be used for stencilling but they take a long time to dry and it is necessary to use a drying agent when working with them. It is not a good idea to flip the stencils over to reverse the design as the paint will not have dried on the stencils and will mark the surface you are working on. The solvent is white spirit.

Alkyd paints

These paints have similar properties to oil paints but they dry more quickly. The solvent is white spirit.

Fabric paints

Usually water-soluble and colour-fixed with a hot iron. Spray paints can also be used for fabrics and produce a very subtle colour effect.

Non-toxic paints

These are worth considering when decorating children's items and are specifically recommended as being safe for toys. Check with your stockist for manufacturers. Wax crayons and wax in small pots are very popular, especially with beginners. The wax crayon has an outer skin or seal which can be broken by rubbing onto a piece of card. The crayon is then rubbed onto the card releasing the wax and the colour taken onto a stencil brush. Because so little of the wax is taken up, they produce a very soft effect and are less likely to creep under the stencil, thereby producing a professional-looking result. They are very easy to use.

> ### WARNING
> When stencilling surfaces or items for children – furniture, toys, walls, fabric etc, – it is essential to use lead-free, non-toxic paints.

Gold waxes and gold varnishes

A wide variety of gold, pewter and silver colours is available, all of which add to the richness of a design. The solvent for these is white spirit. Bronze powders add extra depth and sparkle when sprinkled into the varnish.

Paints for stencilling onto ceramics

There are now water-soluble paints available which are made more durable by baking in the oven.

Glass paints

There are a number of these ranging from water-soluble paints through gels which produce an effect like Tiffany glass, spray paints which produce a frosted or etched-glass effect and paints which give a stained-glass effect.

Traditional paints

These are water-based paints made in a traditional way with a high chalk content but with modern binders. They are my personal favourite, especially for folk art designs as the colours are so good. They dry quickly to a chalky finish. They need sealing at each stage with water-based varnish but both paint and varnish dry extremely quickly. These paints are very good for rubbing through several layers to create a mellow, period look.

Because of the number of different paints available the above is only a general selection. Materials with different properties are coming onto the market all the time. The projects in this book use a variety of materials. Experiment until you find the paint which suits you best and which is the most appropriate for the piece of work you are producing. Look around craft shops, market fairs and decorating merchants for new and interesting materials.

COLOUR
mixing

If you plan to build up your own collection of paints you could start with a basic palette from which you can mix together most of the colours you will need for colour matching. Here is a suggestion to start you off.

- Allow for two of each of the primary colours, alizarin crimson or napthol crimson, both of which have a bias towards mauve.
- Cadmium red which has a bias towards orange.
- Ultramarine blue which has a bias towards mauve.
- Monestial or Prussian blue which have a bias towards green.
- Lemon or azlemon which has a bias towards green.
- Cadmium yellow which has a bias towards orange.

If you mix together the colours which have a bias towards each other you will obtain a clear, bright secondary colour. The earth colours are also useful. Yellow ochre is a soft yellow, which tones down other colours. Raw umber, a greenish dark brown, has a softening effect on other colours, and antiques some of them. It can be used to give a softening wash over finished work. Burnt umber can be mixed with ultramarine blue to produce a rich, dark colour to substitute black, which tends to deaden and dull other colours. White softens all the above colours and turns some of them into pastel or 'ice-cream' colours (always add the colour to white rather than the other way round). In time you will want to add to this list but in the meantime get yourself thoroughly acquainted with this basic palette. Sometimes I do not mix the colours before using them but lay them out separately on my palette (I mix colours on a white ceramic tile as it shows up the colours clearly and is easy to clean). I then mix the paints by adding them to each other on my brush as I go along. For instance, if I am planning to stencil leaves, I lay out one or two yellows, blue and raw umber, taking them onto my brush in turn. These then produce a variety of hues within the stencil. This is, however, a matter of personal choice and, if you prefer, you can mix up the colours with a separate brush on the tile then take up the mixture onto your stencil brush as a single colour.

If you are matching colours to a design on a piece of fabric, try and work in clear daylight if possible. Having gained experience by practising different combinations with the above colours so you are familiar with how they react to each other when mixed, you can carry on experimenting until you find you are approaching the colour that you see on the fabric. Remember that most fabric designs are made up of a number of colours mixed

Before stencilling an item, experiment with a colour scheme to see if the colours work well together.

together, frequently softened by adding raw umber or white or even dulled with a little black. When you feel that you have reached the right hue make a note of the colours you have used. Test a small amount on paper and allow it to dry before going ahead as colours change slightly when they dry. When you are ready, you can mix up enough paint for the whole job in a small glass pot with a screw lid; the paint should last until you need it. Colours have the ability to create a mood, something you should bear in mind if you plan to decorate a whole room. Blues are generally considered cool colours which can make the walls recede, creating a feeling of space. Neutrals made from earth colours are calming. Reds are warm and give an enclosed cocoon-like feeling, bringing the walls in. Greens are restful and yellows can be sunny, cheerful and welcoming. When stencilling a design it is best to keep your colours within the same tonal range in order to create a harmonious whole. Try to avoid having one colour much brighter than the rest, especially if you are planning a border to run around the walls of a room, as one bright colour among soft colours could give the overall appearance an uneven look which could be visually irritating. Remember, too, that colours change in different lights and, where possible (especially if you are planning a border round a room), make a sample of several repeats in the colour you plan to use, ideally on a piece of board painted with the background colour so you can see the effect this has on the colours you are planning to stencil. You can also see how the design itself is going to flow. Place your sample board in different parts of the room and see how the changing light affects it. Consult reference books for ideas, once you have decided on the look you are trying to achieve. Ultimately the choice of colours is very personal. If you are really keen to try a particular combination, even using shades from different tonal ranges, then go for it, as no advice will make up for the experience gained by seeing your ideas followed through.

sources of
INSPIRATION
for stencil designs

As you begin to get some idea of how you want your decorations to look, you will find yourself gradually building up a scrapbook of inspirational ideas which will help you when you come to design your own stencils. These ideas will be individual to you and will help you to make your work personal and original. I keep a folder of postcards which I collect from museums and exhibitions when I see something that might be useful. Wrapping paper, newspaper and magazine cuttings all find their way into plastic sleeves which are then made into a folder. Photographs can be useful to remind you how a particular flower or animal looks, as can natural history books and flower encyclopaedias. Second-hand bookshops can also be worth visiting for old decorating books. Magazines usually have a design section, which can stimulate ideas. Embroidery work is perfect for stencil designs, just as stencil designs can be used as templates for embroidery projects. Once you start looking you will become aware of the immense amount of visual material around you, on which you can base your own designs.

If you enjoy drawing, some of the nicest stencils can be made from the observation of natural objects from life. Ivy can make an excellent design: first sketch the way it grows, then the way the leaves develop from the stem and how this coils round, and then simplify the shapes for transfer onto a stencil. Flowers with their leaves can be drawn from life and then the image simplified for use in stencils. Contents of stately homes and historical houses can produce a folder full of ideas, such as carved wooden embellishments, old wallpapers, porcelain patterns, soft furnishing, statues and urns. Sometimes a small item of architectural decoration such as a bargeboard design can inspire you to turn the pattern into a stencil. There are some lovely designs embossed on old damask tablecloths, clearly visible if you hold them up to the light. As you become more familiar with stencilling, you will find that certain images seem to translate especially well to the stencil medium such as baskets, certain fruits and flowers and so on. By studying the work of the early stencillers you can gain some idea of the simplicity that makes so many of their designs appealing today.

DESIGNING
and CUTTING
your own stencils

Apart from the stencils at the end of this book which accompany the various projects, there are literally hundreds of stencils available for sale as well as books of cut-and-use stencils but, for me, the most enjoyable part of the whole stencilling process and the thing which has continued to enthral me is the designing and cutting of stencils to suit the piece of work I plan to create. The photocopier has completely transformed the way in which stencil design can be worked out, because you

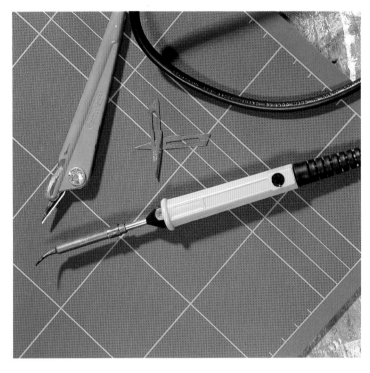

can blow up or reduce a design to see how it will look when made larger or smaller, saving hours of valuable working time. When cutting out a stencil either from card or acetate the design has to be held in place at certain points by strips or bridges. These separate the shapes within the stencil and form an integral part of the design. Without them the stencil would literally fall apart. Part of the skill in producing a satisfactory stencil is to arrange the linking ties or bridges in such a way that they actually form part of the design. If for instance you want to draw a bulrush with long, spear-shaped leaves, cutting out such a long shape would result in a

floppy stencil that is difficult to handle. To overcome this, but still give the impression that you are looking at a long thin leaf you can design a second leaf cutting across it so that the shape where the two leaves cross is divided into two, thus strengthening it. Another device is to have the leaf turn back on itself. In Figure 1 you will see a bulrush shape with the two leaves. If you were to cut these out you would have great difficulty in managing the resulting strips of card and the stencil would be very weak. In addition, the paint would be more likely to run under the stencil.

Figure 1

In Figure 2 the left leaf has cut across the right and also turned back on itself dividing the leaves and the bulrush so that the bridges are formed as part of the design, the actual shapes cut out are smaller and the stencil stronger. As you gain more practice in designing your own stencils you will discover other ways of

Figure 2

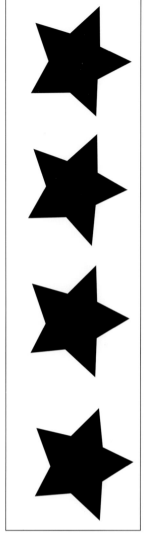

Figure 3

working out the bridges. Stencils can either be positive, where the shapes are cut out and the background to be decorated is covered by the stencil plate (Figure 3), or negative in which the background is cut away leaving the actual design uncut (Figure 4). When you paint onto a negative stencil the shape of the design is shown by the background colour. This is shown in the back view of the Soft Toy project (see page 75) where the apron, bow and ties are not cut away. One type of stencil with no bridges or ties was the Therom stencilling practised on velvet, usually baskets of fruit or flowers, worked in America in the early part of the nineteenth century. These were made up of several stencils, each representing different colours in the design which were laid one over the other and cut so accurately that when they had been stencilled through there was no gap at all between the shapes so that they looked as if they had been painted.

Figure 4

With the use of acetate it is possible to make several stencils for a single design, by separating the colours on each stencil. Because the acetate is transparent it is possible to see through to the previous stencilling, so all the colours are 'clean' and separate. All of the stencils in this book are designed as a single unit with the exception of the ice-cream cone and the tree on top of the Toy Box (see page 95), so that the colours can gently overlap giving a feeling of warmth and unity to the finished design.

To work out your own design

ONE

The example given here is taken from a book of copyright-free designs from Turkey. Having selected the image that appeals to you it needs to be made larger. The obvious solution is to have the design blown up on a photocopier to a practical size, bearing in mind that the shapes will have to be large enough to cut out and that the bridges should be strong enough to hold the design together. If you do not have access to a photocopier you can enlarge the design manually by the grid method. Trace the design onto a piece of paper and draw a grid across the paper of 2 cm (1 in) squares. On a second piece of paper draw a second grid of larger squares: if, for instance, you want to double

the size of the design make the squares double the size of those you drew on the first grid. Copy the original tracing onto the second piece of paper, making sure that the elements of the larger design appear in the same place in the larger squares as in the small ones.

TWO

Whichever method you use, when your design is the size that you wish, take a fine artist's brush and dark ink and work out where you plan to make the breaks or bridges, blocking in the shapes. You should finish with a dark design on the white paper background with the design worked out in separate shapes. You are now ready to draw out your stencil either on stencil card or acetate. For card, take a piece of oiled Manila stencil card allowing approximately 2 cm (1 in) all around the outside of the stencil design. If you make the size any smaller your brush will go over the end of your stencil plate marking your work when you come to stencil. Lay a piece of carbon paper over the card, making sure it covers the whole area to be traced. Lay the blocked-out design over this and fix in place with masking tape so that

your work does not move while you are tracing it. Using a sharp pencil or ballpoint pen trace around all the shapes. Remove the carbon paper and paper template. Examine the design you have traced onto your card carefully to make sure that all the shapes are well separated and the whole design has a nice flow to it.

THREE

Place the card on to the cutting mat and using a craft knife with a sharp blade cut around the shapes. Try not to overrun the end of the shape or you will cut into the bridges. If you do, you can make a repair by sticking a thin strip of masking tape over the cut on each side of the stencil. When you have cut out all the shapes test out your design on a piece of spare lining paper.

FOUR

If you prefer to make your stencil out of acetate then you'll need a sheet of plate glass, taped around the edges. Lay your blocked-out design under this. Tape the acetate onto the glass over the design and using an electrically heated pen (read the manufacturer's instructions first) run the point of the pen carefully around the shapes. Heated pens have overcome the difficulty of cutting out acetate with a craft knife as a knife is inclined to slip on the glass cutting across the bridges. Repairs can be made in the same way, with a piece of masking tape on each side of the stencil. It is possible to use overhead projector film, which can be used in a photocopier so that your design can be photocopied directly onto the film as shown here, thus eliminating the tracing stage altogether.

Wax stencilling crayons are used here. They are very popular with beginners and are easy to use. Rub the wax crayons briskly onto the corner of the stencil card to break the seal, which stops the wax from drying out. Rub the wax onto the stencil card. Take this onto the bristles of a clean stencil brush, wipe off the excess on a piece of clean kitchen paper and work the brush through the stencil adding more wax to the corner of the card as you need it. The effect is very soft and the wax is less likely to seep under the stencil. Build up your colours gradually working from light colours through to dark. The same method is used for the little pots of wax stencilling cream.

It is important to keep your stencils safe. I have found the most practical way of storing stencils is to make a folder of lining paper stapled across the bottom and sides and to write the name of the design on the outside. They can be stored flat in this way. As your collection of stencils builds up it makes it easier to find the stencils you want to use and prevents them from getting torn.

TROUBLESHOOTING

Inevitably, things can go wrong sometimes, so it is best to know in advance how to cope with a problem. The first rule is, don't panic – there is usually a solution.

- If you are working on a wall always try to keep back some of the paint with which the wall has been painted so you can paint out any drastic mistakes if necessary. If the paint has crept under the stencil touch up afterwards with a fine artist's brush and some of the background paint.

- Try and wipe away errors immediately with the appropriate solvent.

- If the stencil looks too bright and harsh when finished, it can be softened by dabbing your design with a little of the background paint on a damp kitchen cloth, but do this delicately or you may soften away the design altogether.

- When working the worst mistakes usually occur when you are tired, so try to stop before this happens. If you are really unhappy with your work try leaving it overnight. It is surprising how much better things look in the morning and you may see a way of dealing with the difficulty more clearly.

- Prior to stencilling, the groundwork can be given a coat of dead flat (non-gloss) varnish; this is especially important when some time has been spent on a paint effect as a base for the stencilling. Having varnished it, errors can then be wiped away easily with a damp rag.

- Errors on paper and textiles are a little more difficult to deal with. It is possible to wash fabrics to remove errors but is far better to try out the design on a spare piece of cloth first to establish how the fabric reacts to the paint. Small smudges can be concealed by the addition of leaves, flowers and so on.

- Always put down adequate protection if you are working in a furnished room and take care to place any delicate soft furnishings safely out of the way. Set up a working area where you can lay out the materials you plan to use. A large tray with a folding stand can be useful for setting out your equipment. Keep a rubbish bag handy and put soiled kitchen paper and used cloths and rags in it immediately, before they can stain the surroundings.

- Be organized. A tray at the top of a ladder with all your equipment on it, for instance, will stop you from having to run up and down every time you need something.

- Remember that the final effect may sometimes not be what you expected, even if you have planned your project carefully in advance, decided where the stencils should go and worked out the colour matches. Taking photographs of your work is a helpful way of recording what you have done and can also be useful to pinpoint where you may have gone wrong. Sometimes all that is needed is to add more stencils, paint some out or slightly alter some of the colouring.

- If all else fails, bear in mind that even famous artists have rejected some of their work and if you are really not satisfied with the result the whole piece can be painted out and you can start all over again.

TECHNIQUES

Turning corners

Each of the four corners of this frame has each been stencilled to show a different technique for turning corners. Top left: making a neat corner when stencilling round a square can present problems. Here a special design has been made for the corner and the border stencilled up to it on each side. There is also a motif to go at the centre of each side so that the border design can be reversed at this point (see the Picture Frame project page 44).

Top right-hand corner: here the stencil was helped to flow around the corner by blocking out part of the stencil to make it fit, and the stencil was reversed as it turned the corner. This method works well for some designs but not for others. Test it out on the piece of lining paper first.

Bottom right: the border is allowed to run right along to the edge on one side and the other side is butted up to it. This can form a neat solution.

Bottom left: mitring is the method that is most often used for turning corners. Tape a piece of masking tape diagonally from the outer to the inner corner. Stencil the border up to the edge of the tape. Remove the tape and place corner to corner again across the border you have just stencilled. Stencil the second side up to the tape. Remove the tape.

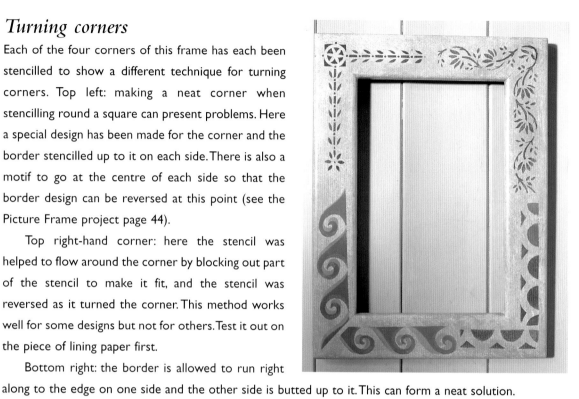

Stencilling with brushes

There is one cardinal rule which applies to brushes, whatever method of stencilling you use: use very little paint and build up the depth of colour gradually. Always keep your brush dry and do not be tempted at any time to dip it into the solvent or the brush will be useless for that particular job until it has been cleaned and dried. Choose a brush which is the right size for the job you are doing and a brush for each colour group. As you add to your equipment it is useful to keep a set of spare brushes. Always clean immediately after use with appropriate solvent.

Method

Dip the stencil brush into the paint up to about 5–6 mm (¼ in) from the end of the bristles. Using a sheet of kitchen paper, wipe most of the paint off the brush until you have only a thin film showing on the paper when it is used. The mark left should be quite soft. If it appears too thick continue to wipe off until you have the right amount. Always test onto lining paper before starting on the item you are going to decorate.

You can apply the paint in different ways. You can use a circular motion starting from the centre of a large shape and working towards the edge. Having fixed your stencil with low tack tape, gently pull the stencil up from the base from time to time to see how the work is going. If there are blobs running under your stencil then your brush is overloaded with paint and should be wiped again on the kitchen paper. You will be surprised at how little paint you need. If the image is very faded, however, you may need a little more paint. Always work from light colours to dark.

Stippling gives your work a grainy look. It is quite a useful technique when working on very small details. Tape 1 cm (½ in) masking tape around the base of the bristles to stiffen the brush and work with a gentle stabbing or stippling motion.

If the shapes are quite large you can produce an interesting effect by dragging the brush sideways across the stencil. To give depth and movement to the design you can add more paint at points where the object would be darker. This works especially well with bows and ribbons, the centre of flowers and so on to define a shape.

Using a marine sponge

Sponges can be used to achieve interesting effects. The Coffee Table project (page 88) shows how one colour has been sponged across a second colour through the stencil.

Stencilling with a mini roller

This method has been described elsewhere (in the Bathroom (see page 110), and with practice it can be a very useful way of covering large areas quickly.

Stencilling with aerosol paints

Spray paints are wonderful to use for stencilling and with a little practice the technique is easily mastered. Lovely subtle and shaded colours can be created to give a pleasing and harmonious effect.

A wide range of aerosol paints is available in every imaginable colour. The great advantage of aerosol paint is that it is very easy to use and requires no cleaning up afterwards or washing dirty brushes. The paint dries almost instantly allowing the stencil to be quickly moved, without fear of smudging. The spraying technique does require some skill, so have a practice session first using an old stencil and newspapers. By using the paint in very thin veils of colour you will soon achieve beautifully shaded and mellow effects.

It is very important to use a re-positional adhesive to stick the stencil to the surface, otherwise the paint will drift over the stencil leaving an unattractive fuzzy outline. Apply the adhesive to the back of the stencil then press the stencil onto the surface, making sure all the edges are securely stuck down. If the stencil does not completely cover the surface to be stencilled, mask round the edge of the stencil with kitchen paper and low tack masking tape. This will prevent the spray from drifting over the edge of the stencil and leaving an unsightly and indelible mark. When you have chosen the colours you plan to use always try out a sample first to ensure the result is what you are trying to achieve.

Hold the aerosol about 15 cm (6 in) away from the surface of the stencil and with a gentle pumping action use short bursts of spray. It is important to use the paint very sparingly. Too much paint will result in a muddy and heavy effect that cannot be corrected. If the surface becomes too wet the paint will seep under the edge of the stencil and spoil the outline of the design.

Remember that the stencilled image will always look stronger when you lift the stencil, so don't be afraid to peep under the edge of the stencil from time to time to assess your progress. Don't worry if there is a slight variation of colour and shading: a slightly random and soft-edged look is always pleasing. If the resulting work looks too slick or strongly coloured it can be knocked back by lightly sanding or ragging over with a thin wash of paint. This looks wonderful on old or uneven surfaces. Stencilled fabric cannot be adjusted in this way, however, so it is important to be sure of your technique.

WARNING

Always read the instructions on the can very carefully and follow the manufacturer's recommendations. To avoid inhaling the vapour always wear a mask and protect your eyes with goggles. Disposable masks may be used if the work is to be quickly completed. For more time-consuming projects invest in a rubber mask with good filters. Always work in a well-ventilated area even outside or in a garage with the doors open. When stencilling anything that is to be used by children always check with the manufacturers that the paint is safe. If you are pregnant it is best to avoid aerosols altogether.

PAPER

There are a number of possibilities for stencilling designs onto paper and this section will give you some ideas on which you can build. Handmade greetings cards are always welcome, because they are very personal, and they show that the sender has taken trouble. On a practical note, it is useful to be able to produce a card at short notice knowing that the design has already been worked out. I have suggested suitable paints for working on the individual projects but wax crayons and small pots of waxes, which are readily available, are also especially suitable for paperwork. They are very easy to use and produce excellent results even for beginners. One thing to remember about working on paper, particularly when decorating cards, is that it is extremely difficult to remove errors without leaving any trace, so you do need to work on a clean, grease-free surface and keep your hands clean and free of paint. It is a good idea to try out your stencil on spare sheets of paper or card first to perfect your design.

Experiment with different types and weights of paper before embarking on an actual project to see what effect different background colours and textures can have on your stencilling.

Some papers have a slightly mottled finish and these make a perfect background for stencilling. Some of the designs would be equally effective worked on other surfaces, such as the Christmas Tablecloth (page 39). Having finished your work, lay it flat or store it in a folder to prevent it from becoming creased. If the worst happens and your work does become damaged you can then reproduce it faithfully by using your original stencil once again.

JAM POT
covers & labels

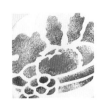

For those who enjoy making their own preserves, an attractive way to present the fruits of your labours is to hand-decorate labels and covers. The labels double up as bookplates or, if enlarged, the design can act as a border for menu cards.

Designer's liquid acrylics that come in a small pot with a dropper, are used for this project. These paints are particularly suitable for working on paper, as the consistency is just right and you can control the amount of paint dispensed with the dropper. They are not recommended for projects requiring large quantities of paint.

YOU WILL NEED

- non-permanent repositional glue
- stencil (template page 122)
- plain lightweight cartridge paper for the covers
- designer's liquid acrylic colour in ultramarine blue, bright yellow, crimson red, spectrum red (bright red)
- white tile
- 3 stencil brushes, taped around the base of the bristles with masking tape
- kitchen cloth
- a brush for mixing colours
- pinking shears (optional)
- elastic band
- narrow ribbon
- ready-gummed labels 78 x 116 mm (3 x 4½ in)

ONE
To make the pot covers, lightly roll the non-permanent glue across the back of the stencil. Position the stencil on the paper. Drop a few drops of ultramarine blue paint onto the tile. Using one of the prepared stencil brushes take up the paint, and remove the excess on the kitchen cloth. Lightly tap or stipple the brush over the border and bowl shapes without moving the stencil.

TWO
Drop a few drops of bright yellow next to the blue and mix up a green for the leaves. As you have already stencilled all the blue areas you can use the same brush to stipple the green onto the leaves.

THREE

Drop some ultramarine paint
and some crimson onto a
clean part of the tile. When
you have mixed this use the
second brush to stipple the
grapes. Add a little more blue
to your stencil brush to
stipple in the deeper shade of
the plum.

FOUR

Mix together the bright red
and yellow to make orange
and stipple over the image.
Lift off the stencil and cut
round the paper. You can use
pinking shears to give an
attractive finish.

*All manner of attractive
labels and covers can be
produced, by using a
different stencil design
and a new combination
of colours.*

SIX

Remove the stencil and trim
up to the stencilled border. Fix
your work to the top of the
jam jar with an elastic band
and cover this with a narrow
ribbon if you wish.

FIVE

Stencil the label in the same
way using blue for the edge,
red for the cherries and green
for the leaves.

GIFT-WRAP

A gift can be made more special by using hand-decorated wrapping paper. Ordinary brown wrapping paper can lend itself to a number of decorative possibilities. Gold stencilling across the faintly striped brown of the paper can be very effective, particularly for Christmas presents; tie the gift with gold ribbon, or try coloured raffia for a stylish and elegant effect. By decorating your own gift-wrap you can incorporate specific, highly personal motifs which relate to the occasion or the interests of the recipient. In this project by first colouring and then stencilling the paper – you can produce something that is both original and personal.

YOU WILL NEED

- brown wrapping paper
- 1½ inch paint brush
- large wooden board
- gummed paper strip
- acrylic paints: monestial blue, monestial green and gold
- white tile
- kitchen cloth
- bronze powder
- re-positional adhesive
- stencils (press-out supplied)
- 2 stencil brushes
- kitchen paper
- wide ribbon – choose a colour that will co-ordinate with the gift-wrap – I have used golden yellow here
- ruler
- pencil
- blank card suitable for decorating (e.g. a small sheet of cartridge paper, folded)
- hole punch
- thin ribbon that will co-ordinate with the card – golden yellow was used here

ONE
To get the paper to lie flat, wet the paper on both sides, lay onto the wooden board allowing a margin of wooden board all round the paper, gently smooth into place and tape around the edges with the gummed paper strip.

TWO
Allow to dry. Check that it has dried smooth and taut. Leave the gummed paper in place until you have completed the stencilling.

TECHNIQUES USED

❋ stretching paper for painting
❋ registering and stencilling a half drop pattern
❋ simple ragging
❋ shadowing

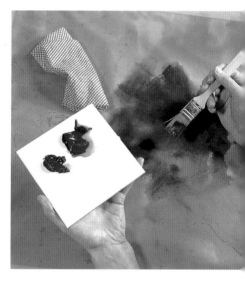

THREE
Squeeze about 3 cm (1¼ in) monestial blue acrylic paint onto the white tile and using plenty of water quickly paint all over the paper, dabbing with a kitchen cloth as you go. Then squeeze out about 3 cm (1¼ in) monestial green and work this into the damp background, again dabbing with the kitchen cloth to soften the marks and to allow the blue to show through here and there. Do not worry if the paper appears to swell and wrinkle again as it will become flat as it dries. Allow to dry overnight.

FOUR

To stencil the all-over pattern squeeze about 3 cm (1¼ in) gold acrylic paint onto a clean white tile and add a little bronze powder for added sparkle. Working from the top left-hand side, lay the stencil down – you cannot use tape to fix the stencil as you will tear the paper but instead use non-permanent repositional glue on the back. Mix together the bronze powder and gold paints with a brush and take up the mixture onto the end of a clean stencil brush. Work off the excess onto the kitchen paper and paint through the stencil. Make sure you stencil in the registration mark to the right, which will help you with the positioning, when you come to the next row across.

FIVE

Continue down the row placing the little heart shape at the top of the stencil over the little heart shape at the bottom of the newly painted stencil. Work your way down to the bottom of the paper in this way using the little heart shape as registration. For the next row position the stencil so that the leaf registration to the left covers the leaf mark which you made to the right of the design as you worked the first row. This should form a half-drop repeat pattern, so that as you work across the paper you will see that four large hearts form a diamond shape.

SIX

The same stencil is used to decorate the ribbon with the shapes at the sides blanked out to make the design fit the ribbon. In the press-outs at the back of the book you will find that this has already been done for you. Measure the width of the ribbon and make a mark each side of the stencil the same width as the ribbon.

SEVEN

Squeeze a little blue and green paint onto the tile repeating the method used for the wrapping paper. Match the top small heart to the bottom small heart on the previous shape as you work down making sure that the pencil marks on the stencil are in line with the sides of the ribbon.

EIGHT

To make a greetings card to match, stencil a heart onto the front of the blank card lightly in green just below the centre point and slightly to the right.

NINE

Slide the stencil up and to the left and paint over part of the original shape in blue. This technique is called shadowing and can be used to give a three-dimensional effect. Punch holes in the card and tie with thin gold ribbon.

VARIATION

Stars make an excellent motif. Try decorating the parcel with a contrasting coloured ribbon, also decorated with stars.

LAMPSHADE

Decorated paper lampshades are very attractive and quick to make. With the help of a special brass fitting to support them they can be cut to any size and may be stencilled with a design to suit a particular theme – Christmas, a birthday, a romantic Valentine's dinner or an anniversary. Shades for bedside lamps can be decorated to blend in with the soft furnishings, perhaps taking a single flower from a floral pattern on the curtains and turning it into a stencil. The possibilities are infinite. The template shown here allows the bottom edge to be straight or scalloped. It is important when your work is finished to use a fire-retardant spray and do not allow the light bulb to come into contact with the paper shade.

YOU WILL NEED

- stiff card 250 gms weight in the colour of your choice (cream is used here)
- pencil
- stencil (template page 123)
- non-permanent glue
- designer's liquid acrylic paints used here (ultramarine blue, bright yellow, bright red, white, monestial blue, lemon yellow) but most acrylic paints would be suitable
- white tile
- 4 stencil brushes
- kitchen paper
- scissors
- PVA glue
- 2 paper clips
- fire-retardant spray
- brass fitting for electric light
- light stand

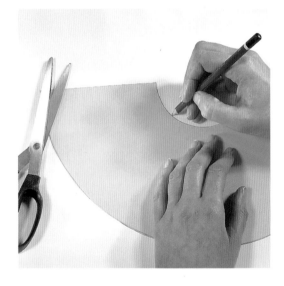

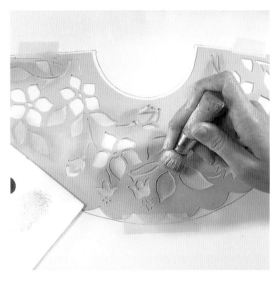

ONE
Draw round the template onto the card. The template is a little larger than the stencil given to allow a narrow margin at the top, which will be stencilled as a fine borderline as shown.

TWO
Run the non-permanent glue around the edge of the back of the stencil. Fix the stencil in position over the traced outline, allowing for the small margin at the top as described. Squeeze a little ultramarine blue and bright yellow paint onto the white tile. Mix these for the leaves and stalks. Take up the paint onto the tip of the stencil brush and wipe off the excess on the kitchen paper. Stencil all the leaves and the stalks.

THREE

Leave the stencil in place and mix together bright red, bright yellow and white on a clean part of the tile. Add the red and yellow to the white, not the other way round. When you have achieved a soft apricot colour, take up the paint with a clean stencil brush and, having wiped off the excess paint on kitchen paper, stencil in all the flowers using a circular movement with your brush. Stencil the tips of any buds as well. Now dip your brush just into the bright red. Do not do this too enthusiastically, as you do not want the colour to be too bright. Wipe off the excess on kitchen paper and stipple the centre of each flower only.

TECHNIQUES USED

* making a card lampshade
* simple colour mixing
* using the template to define the line at the top and scallops at the base of the lamp
* stencilling multi-colours through the same stencil

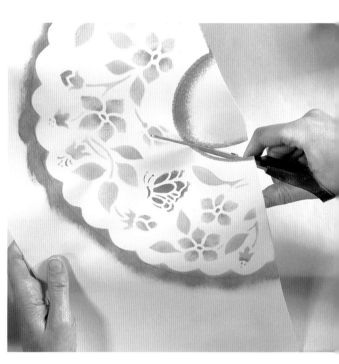

FOUR

Still leaving the stencil in place stencil the butterfly. Starting with the white paint, add a little lemon yellow and very gradually a little monestial blue – this should make a delicate blue-green. Using the third brush stencil the butterfly with this mix, and finally add a very little of just the monestial blue onto the same brush and use this to define the edges of the butterfly's wings. Stencil the scallops up to the edge of the template and the margin at the top with this colour as well.

FIVE

Making sure the paint is dry, cut out the shape.

SIX

Paste a thin line of glue down the seam and position the other end of the shade over this. While the glue is drying keep the seam in position with a paper clip fixed at the top and bottom. Finally spray over the whole shade with fire-retardant spray.

VARIATION

The lampshade can be decorated to co-ordinate with any room, or any occasion. This lamp could be part of a decorative Christmas table.

CHRISTMAS
tablecloth

I have used a paper tablecloth for this stencilling project but if you wish to make something a little more permanent, a large white sheet would be suitable. The procedure is the same but fabric paints would need to be used. The important thing is to measure the piece of paper or cloth in order to put the stencils in the right place. Although a cloth decorated for a Christmas meal is shown, there are a whole host of occasions when a decorated cloth would be appropriate, including weddings, birthdays, and anniversaries. The galleon design could be used on a child's toy or, evenly spaced, on ceramic tiles in a bathroom. The holly wreaths could be stencilled onto a window or door panel during the festive season. The holly can be used on napkins to match the tablecloth, round a Christmas apron or on wrapping paper. A word of warning – as you are working on a large area make sure you keep all your painting equipment on a separate small table and, to avoid spillages do not succumb to the temptation to sit them on top of your work while decorating.

YOU WILL NEED

- a white paper tablecloth or sheet
- tailor's marking chalk
- a pair of compasses
- stencil (templates pages 124–25 and press-outs supplied)
- extra card to use for template and marker
- re-positional non-permanent adhesive
- acrylic paint in copper/gold, dark green and bright red
- 3 stencil brushes
- kitchen paper
- white tile
- thumbtack
- tape measure

ONE

Find the centre of the tablecloth and mark it lightly with the tailor's chalk. If you are using a sheet, fold it in half then iron a crease along the fold and repeat the other way. Where the creases bisect is the centre. Lay the cloth out flat on a large, clean flat surface.

TWO

The design of this cloth illustrates the Christmas carol *I Saw Three Ships*. As an alternative, a Christmas bell can replace the galleons. The galleon is designed to decorate the centre of the cloth and in order to fit in the three ships a circle with a radius of 9 cm (3½ in) is drawn with the compasses on a template. The centre of the circle matches the centre of the tablecloth. The circle is divided equally into three points and the bottom of these points shows where the ships are to go. Cover the back of the stencil with re-positional adhesive (you cannot use tape, as it would tear the paper).

THREE

Shake the pot of gold paint, unscrew the lid and dip the stencil brush directly into the lid of the pot and wipe off the excess on kitchen paper. Using a circular motion stencil the entire ship except for the flag.

FOUR

Drop a few drops of bright red paint onto the white tile and with the second brush stencil in the flag. Remove the stencil, leaving the template in place, and position the ship stencil under the second point on the circle. Stencil this in the same way and when this is complete move to the third point and stencil the third ship. With the gold paint and the star stencil decorate around the base of the ships.

FIVE

Next decorate the holly circle. The holly stencil forms exactly half a circle and there is a dot to show the centre. Measure how far the centre of this circle is to go from the centre of the cloth. Make a note of this measurement so that all the other circles are stencilled the same distance from the centre. Use a point between the two ships for guidance as shown on the template. The position of the other three circles is worked out just below the ships. Place a thumbtack through the point marking the centre of the stencil. Using the third brush and dark green paint, paint in the top half of the holly wreath, stencil the leaves dark green and the berries bright red. When this has been completed, pivot the stencil round keeping the thumbtack in place and stencil the bottom half. A total of six circles are worked in this way.

SEVEN

Using the holly and ribbon stencils work out where the corner pieces are to go, stencil the holly in dark green, the berries and the ribbon in red. You can also centre sprigs of holly and ribbon around the cloth, 5 cm (2 in) from the edge. Sprinkle the corners with stars.

SIX

Because the wording of the carol is to be repeated it is better to cut out the whole sentence onto stencil card so that the spacing can be adjusted on the stencil card. It would be very difficult to make alterations on the tablecloth. On the stencil card draw a line across the base about 1 cm (½ in) from the edge. Using this as a guide and using the alphabet stencils, stencil the message across the strip. Decide how far from the edge the message is to go and make a template to attach to the base which exactly comes to the edge of the tablecloth. Using the crease marking the centre of each side, centre the wording and position the stencil. Stencil the letters in bright red.

TECHNIQUES USED

* stencilling a paper tablecloth
* working out measurements
* finding the centre
* using a stencil alphabet

WOOD

Stencilling looks effective against the natural grain of pine. Water-based wood stains can also be used cleverly to suggest marquetry, and small sample pots of different colours of wood stain can be bought, which would be eminently suitable for stencilling.

Plain white can look stark because the bridges of the stencil already break up the designs, so soften the background with sponging.

Small wooden objects such as waste paper baskets, picture frames, small sets of shelves and so on, nowadays often made in medium density fibreboard (MDF), are easy to decorate quickly and effectively and require little of the tiring preparation work required for similar pieces made in wood as they have a smooth surface and no knots. MDF has certainly revolutionised decorative painting from this point of view but a slight disadvantage of this material is that it is not always as resistant to knocks as wood and will bruise if treated roughly. If sawing or sanding MDF always wear a protective mask to avoid inhaling the fine dust thrown up. To make life easier when decorating I usually suggest removing lids, doors, drawers, and so on, where possible, taking care not to let paint build up too thickly along the edges of these, as they will not shut properly when replaced if this happens.

It is possible that the piece you are about to work on has already been painted, so all that is needed is a wipe with a damp cloth and a little detergent so that it will accept the stencil paint. When working on small objects it is best to leave a space around your design so the final effect is not too cramped, and to try and keep your design in scale with the piece you are working on.

PICTURE
frame

Choosing the right frame can greatly enhance the picture it is to contain. Photographs, paintings, certificates and even favourite postcards can all be made to look far more impressive if some thought is given to their framing. Mirrors, too, can look dramatic with a decorative border. Attractive frames can be expensive to buy but many shops stock a large variety of relatively cheap wooden frames which are suitable for decoration.

You can also make your own frame to the size and shape you want by using a mitring device. For this project a square piece of 1 cm (½ in) thick MDF was used, from which a square was cut out from the centre appropriate to the size of the picture. When cutting or sanding MDF you should always wear a mask. To this a narrow moulding around the outer and inner edges was attached – the inner moulding also formed the rebate to hold the picture.

YOU WILL NEED

- wood filler
- sandpaper
- red oxide coloured emulsion paint
- 2 cm (1 in) paint brush
- household candle
- matt black emulsion paint
- fine wire wool
- a piece of paper
- white chalk
- ball point pen
- low tack masking tape
- stencils (press-outs provided)
- gold varnish
- stencil brush
- white spirit
- gold wax
- dead flat acrylic varnish

TWO
Rub over raised areas of moulding with the household candle to act as a resist for the next layer of paint. Don't do this too vigorously, as the finished effect should be subtle.

ONE
Fill in any nail marks or cracks with wood filler and allow to dry. Wearing a protective mask, sand down. Paint the whole of the frame with red oxide coloured emulsion and allow to dry.

THREE
Paint over the whole frame with matt black emulsion and allow to dry. Rub over the raised sections of the moulding with fine wire wool. The paint over the areas rubbed with the candle will come away revealing the red paint underneath.

FOUR

To stencil, first find the centre of each side. Cut a piece of paper the exact length and width of the flat surface of the long and short sides. Fold this in half lengthways and open out. Rub the chalk over the back of the paper. Lay the long strip of paper over the corresponding side of the frame and draw over the fold with a ballpoint pen, and the chalk backing will make a mark on the frame showing where the centre is. Using the shorter piece of paper, repeat the process with the short side of the frame. Mark all four sides in this way.

FIVE

Using the low tack tape to position the stencil, first stencil each corner using the corner stencil and the gold varnish. Shake the varnish bottle well and when you remove the lid you can dip your brush into the varnish which remains in the lid. Any corrections can be made with white spirit. When all the corners have been completed start with the first long side. Taking the border stencil, place the daisy centre over the chalk mark and stencil up to the corner having first covered the corner with a small piece of card. Turn the stencil over, and stencil up to the second corner. Repeat for all four sides.

SIX

Dip your finger into the gold wax and rub round the inner and outer edgings of the mouldings. To protect your work, finish with a coat of dead flat acrylic varnish.

GARDEN
trug

This trug has a prettily shaped handle and when bought it was in bare pine. As a contrast to working with medium density fibreboard which has a perfectly smooth surface I wanted to retain the 'woody' look of this item, which I felt would be an appropriate background to the rustic theme with which I planned to stencil it. I first soaked the whole trug in a bowl of water to raise the grain of the wood and then allowed it to dry. I then prepared it by filling in any nail holes with wood filler, sanding down any rough edges caused through the original sawing but leaving any small imperfections in the wood itself. The whole trug was then sealed with a coat of sanding sealer and any knots in the pine sealed with knotting to avoid resin leaking from them with the passage of time.

YOU WILL NEED

- sample pot bright blue emulsion, latex or traditional paint, 250 ml (8 fl oz)
- sample pot egg-yolk yellow emulsion, latex or traditional paint, (250 ml (8 fl oz)
- dead-flat acrylic varnish
- stencils (templates page 126 and press-out supplied)
- acrylic paints ('golden' acrylic paints which are particularly suitable for stencilling were used) in white, yellow, burnt umber, black, dark green, bright red and grey
- low tack tape
- 4 stencil brushes
- 3 cm (1¼ in) paint brush
- white tile
- fine artist's brush
- lining paper

ONE
Paint two coats of blue on the outside of the trug. When this is dry paint the inside with bright yellow. When the paint is completely dry, cover all painted surfaces with the dead-flat acrylic varnish. To decorate the handle I have used part of the stencil for the Gift-wrap project (see press-outs). Position the stencil with the low tack tape. Stencil the daisy shapes in bright red and the leaves in dark green, leaving the stencil in place as you work.

TWO
Reverse the stencil and decorate underneath the handle working out your design as you go along. When this is complete, using the artist's brush, fill in the centre of the flowers with bright yellow paint.

THREE
Decide where the various elements given on the goose stencil sheet in the back of the book will be placed. I have used the corn each end of the sides. Stencil this in bright yellow and then lightly dip your stencil brush in burnt umber and stencil the base of the corn with this. Reverse the stencil and place it at the other end of the side.

FOUR

Decide where the first goose is to be placed. Position the stencil with low tack tape. Stencil the whole shape in white first, lifting the wing flap, which has been attached with tape at the top of the goose.

TECHNIQUES USED

❀ preparation of bare pine for stencilling

❀ making up a scene using several stencils

❀ stencilling in birds' wings

❀ variation on the original stencil for the Gift-wrap project (see page 33)

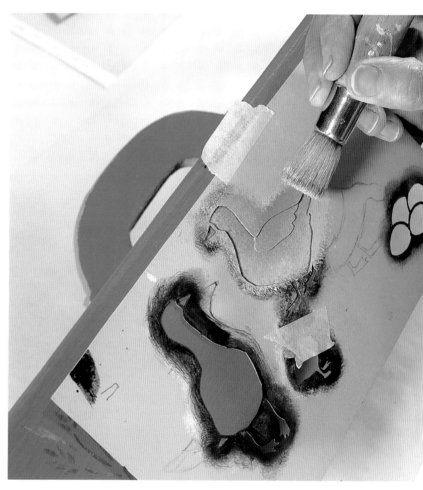

FIVE

Lay the wing flap down onto the goose and stencil over this with the grey colour, using a stippling motion. Leaving the stencil in place, and using the brush with yellow paint, stencil in the beak and feet. When this has been finished, lift off the stencil and mark the eye with a black dot using the fine artist's brush. Continue in this way to stencil in any other geese. The goslings will work the same way using yellow instead of white for their bodies.

VARIATION

The stencils can be enlarged and used as a template for embroidery, first stretching the embroidery canvas onto a board and using a single-colour fabric paint which is heat-sealed to prevent the paint leaking onto the embroidery thread. This would make a nice theme for a child's cotton bib or apron.

SIX

Using the stencil brush with dark green paint and the grass stencil, stencil in a horizon at the back, taking care not to overlap the geese already painted. Finish with a coat of varnish. You can vary the scene shown using the various elements provided. If you are unsure as to what the end result will look like, experiment first on lining paper.

TRAY

Trays lend themselves to a whole range of decorative styles — rustic for garden use, stylish for entertaining, fresh and cheerful for breakfast. The possibilities are endless. Ready-made trays are easily found, often with a white heatproof plastic covered base and a wooden surround, so this is a typical example for decoration.

YOU WILL NEED

- stiff metal brush
- coarse sandpaper
- PVA to paint over the heatproof surface
- fine wire wool
- liming wax
- soft cloth
- clear wax
- latex or emulsion paint (bright blue for the background, bright yellow for the sunflowers, pale yellow and leaf green for the leaves
- water-based dead-flat acrylic varnish
- stencils (templates page 126 and press-outs supplied)
- lining paper
- 5 stencil brushes
- white tile
- acrylic paint in burnt sienna and burnt umber for the centre of the sunflowers. Bright black and red for the ladybird
- brush for mixing
- small piece of bubble wrap
- water-based floor-quality varnish
- low-tack masking tape

ONE

Using the stiff metal brush, brush briskly over the pine surround of the tray to open up the grain. Sand down the white base to provide a key for the paint. Give the base a coat of PVA. With the fine wire wool work the liming wax into the pine. Allow 5 minutes to dry then remove the excess with a soft cloth. Finally, apply a coat of clear wax. Paint the base of the tray bright blue. Allow to dry and if necessary apply a second coat of paint. When this is dry paint over a light coat of acrylic varnish.

TWO

Plan where you are going to place your sunflower heads. At this stage you might wish to practice stencilling sunflower heads on the lining paper until you are satisfied with the result. Allowing for the petals round the centre, place the cut-out circle where the centre of the flower is to be and cover it with tape.

THREE
Stencil the petals with the stencil brush using a circular motion. First use the bright yellow and work your way around the circle, overlapping the petals as you go and making sure the base of the petals always comes over the edge of the centre circle.

FOUR
When the petals form a circle, go round once more with the pale yellow. Do not attempt to cover the previous petals but always make sure the base comes a little over the centre circle.

FIVE
To stencil the centre of the flowers remove the card circle and place the card with the circle cut out over the space left in the centre of the petals. On the tile mix together burnt sienna and burnt umber acrylic paint to make a rich brown. Add a little water to thin the mix. Paint the circle keeping a fraction away from the edge to keep the paint from creeping underneath.

TECHNIQUES USED

❊ using liming wax
❊ preparing a plastic,
  heatproof surface for
  decorating
❊ free-stencilling flowers
❊ two-part ladybird stencil
❊ protecting a surface to
  ensure it is heatproof
❊ using bubble wrap to
  create texture

SIX

Quickly lay the bubble wrap
over the wet paint bubble-
side down and press down
firmly. When it is pulled away
it should leave a clear imprint.
Allow to dry. Work the other
sunflower heads in the same
way. Allow to dry.

SEVEN

Taking the leaf stencil, position
the leaf in the spaces around
the sunflowers and stencil
with the green paint, using a
stippling motion stipple up to
the edge of the petals,
checking through the stencil
as you go that you do not
stencil over the petals.

EIGHT

Decide where you want the ladybird to be before you stencil it. Because this is a whole shape with no bridges it can be placed on the flowers over your previous stencilling if you wish. Using the whole shape and bright red acrylic paint stipple over this. Remove the stencil and place the stencil with the dots and legs over the red shape. Using the black paint stipple in the dots and the legs. When all your work is quite dry paint over the whole of the base with at least three coats of floor-quality water-based acrylic varnish, allowing two hours between each coat. This will make the tray tough and heatproof. If you do not want a glossy finish add a final coat of deaf-flat acrylic varnish.

WRITING
slope

A writing slope is an ideal object for decoration. It is very useful to have somewhere to keep writing paper, stamps, postcards etc. all in one place. This one is made of medium density fibreboard ready for decorating which reduces the amount of preparation work, as the surface is already smooth. Because this is quite a small item, I painted the inside as well, finishing it off with the owner's initials inside. As the box is to be decorated inside and out, remove the lid to make it easier to paint. Keep the hinges and screws in a labelled tin. Seal all surfaces with sanding sealer.

YOU WILL NEED

- sample pot old rose pink emulsion or latex paint, 250 ml (8 fl oz)
- 3 cm (1¼ in) paint brush
- fine line tape 3 mm (⅛ in) wide
- sample pot blue-grey emulsion or latex paint, 250 ml (8 fl oz)
- cotton buds
- dead-flat acrylic varnish
- stencil (template page 127 and press-outs supplied)
- lining paper
- low tack masking tape
- acrylic paints in titanium white, raw umber, cadmium red, yellow ochre and ultramarine blue
- brush for mixing
- white tile
- 4 stencil brushes
- fine artist's brush
- dark oak furniture wax
- cotton wool
- soft cloth
- white spirit

ONE
Paint the base and lid inside and out with the pink emulsion. Allow to dry. If necessary apply a second coat and allow to dry.

TWO
Using the fine line tape, run the tape about 1 cm (½ in) away from the edge all round the lid of the box and make sure it is smoothed down. Tape round the outside of the base, crossing the tapes over in the front centre. It is a matter of preference where you would like the lining to be. It is there to define the shape of the box and to contain the stencil design.

THREE
With the blue-grey emulsion, paint over the outside of the lid and the outside of the base, painting over the fine line tape and leaving the inside of the box and the moulding pink. Allow to dry.

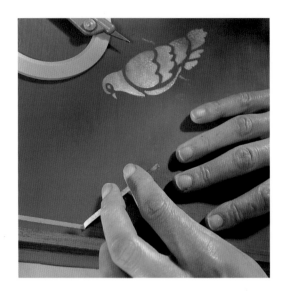

FOUR

Remove the fine line tape and
tidy any paint that has crept
underneath with a damp
cotton bud. Paint a coat of
dead-flat acrylic varnish over
the outside of the lid and
base. Decide where the doves
and the blossom are to be
stencilled. Using the stencils
designed for this project try
out some arrangements on a
piece of lining paper first. Then
position the stencil for the
birds using low tack tape.
Stencil in titanium white first.
Without removing the stencil
make a mix using a little raw
umber with titanium white
and a very little blue to make
a stone colour.

FIVE

Using the stone colour define
the shape of the doves by
working the stencil brush
around the edges of the birds.
With a clean brush stencil the
beaks with yellow ochre.
When the stencil is removed
fill in the eyes with a dark mix
of ultramarine blue and raw
umber with a fine artist's
brush. To stencil the blossom,
mix some titanium white and
a small amount of cadmium
red and yellow ochre on the
tile adding the last two
colours to the titanium white
until you obtain a soft peach
colour. Mix together the
ultramarine blue and yellow
ochre for the leaves on
another part of the tile. Stencil
in the blossom and leaves,
using separate brushes for the
peach and green. As you have
varnished after painting the
base coat, you should be able
to wipe off any errors
immediately with a little
washing-up liquid on a damp
cloth without disturbing
the base.

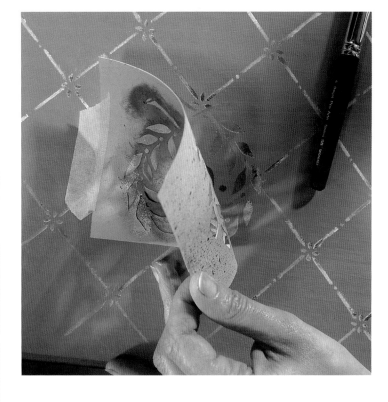

TECHNIQUES USED

❋ lining using masking tape
❋ colour mixing
❋ antiquing using dark wax
❋ using stencils to create a
  small scene

SEVEN

If you wish to stencil the
inside of the lid, do it now. You
may wish to add initials or a
small motif. I chose a
decorative pattern with a
central motif. Varnish with
dead-flat acrylic varnish.
Replace the lid and screw the
hinges back into position.

SIX

Continue adding leaves and
blossoms until you are
satisfied with your
arrangement. Stencil in the
butterfly using the ultramarine
blue mixed with a little
titanium white. When all the
paint has dried coat with dark
oak furniture wax to give a
mellow antique look to your
work. If this appears too dark,
tone down with a little white
spirit on a pad of cotton wool.
Buff to a shine with a soft
cloth.

CERAMICS & GLASS

China responds well to stencilling, but as the surface is slippery it is easier to begin with flat surfaces such as large plates, graduating to more complicated shapes as you gain in practice. Some types of acetate stencils are easier to bend round curved surfaces and it is best to keep the shape simple and not try too much detail. It is a good idea to choose a theme for your china that complements other items. Once heat-cured, decorated china should be dishwasher-safe. A stencilled tile table-top for the garden is another useful idea.

Some lovely effects can be achieved by stencilling onto windows, as a pleasant way of providing a screen and as an alternative to frosted glass.

It is important to ensure that the surface is thoroughly clean and free of grease before stencilling, to allow sufficient time for the paint to cure, and to avoid decorating glass in an area which is subjected to constant damp as this gives rise to condensation and although this can be partially overcome by double glazing after decorating, the paint can eventually slide off. Proprietary window cleaners can damage your work so to protect the paint when cleaning wipe over with a damp cloth only.

Glass paints for stencilling have many possibilities and, as alterations are made so easily, they are fun to experiment with. Allow at least a week for your paints to cure when you have finished your work. It can be cleaned with a little detergent on a soft cloth after that.

CERAMIC
jug

The simple ladybird and leaf stencils used here are intended to complement the Tray project (see page 49). Until fairly recently paint used for painting china was spirit-based to make it adhere well to the china but water-based paints are now available which are less hazardous, more convenient and also quick-drying. You can cure the paints to enamel hardness by baking the finished work in a domestic oven. Brushes can be washed out in water and a little detergent and any corrections necessary can easily be made by wiping off with a damp cotton bud. Once baked your work becomes dishwasher-safe and resistant to wear.

YOU WILL NEED

- latex gloves
- white spirit or denatured alcohol
- cotton wool
- stencils (template page 126 and press-outs supplied)
- low tack masking tape
- cocktail sticks
- a white tile
- water-based ceramic paints in bright red and leaf green (Pebeo Porcelaine 150)
- 3 stencil brushes
- kitchen paper
- relief outliner in anthracite. (This comes in a tube which makes it possible to draw with the paint)

ONE
Wearing protective latex gloves, clean and degrease all surfaces to be decorated with white spirit or denatured alcohol on cotton wool. This will help the paint to stick to the slippery surface.

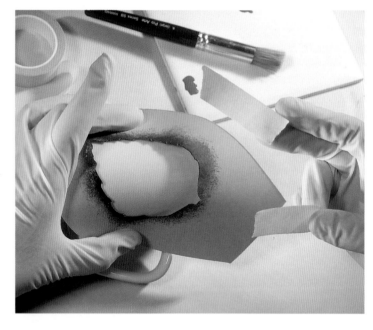

TWO
Position the leaf stencil where you want it to be, using low tack masking tape. With a cocktail stick decant a few drops of the green paint onto the white tile just before you are ready to use it as the paint dries quickly. Take up the paint onto the tip of your stencil brush. Remove surplus paint onto kitchen paper and stencil the leaf using a stippling motion. Just before the paint is dry use the point of a cocktail stick to mark out the veins. Allow the paint to dry for 10 minutes as the ladybird is going to overlap the leaf and you do not wish to disturb the first coat of green paint.

TECHNIQUES
USED

❀ working with water-based
   ceramic paints
❀ texturing (working in the
   leaf veins)

THREE

Following the same
procedure, fix the ladybird
base stencil in position
overlapping the leaf and
decant a few drops of the red
paint onto the tile. With a
clean stencil brush stencil the
ladybird in red and remove
the stencil. Allow to dry.

FOUR

Squeeze a small amount of
relief outliner onto the tile.
Fix the spot stencil over the
red base of the ladybird and
with the third brush stencil in
the spots. Remove the stencil.
Because the stencil is so small
and the surface slippery it is
easier to draw in the legs
free-hand with the relief
outliner. You can practise with
the outliner on the tile
beforehand until you feel you
are able to control the flow.
Finally leave your work to air-
dry for 24 hours then place in
a cold oven. Set the oven to
150°C/300°F/Gas Mark 2 and
when the required heat has
been reached set a timer for
35 minutes. When baked turn
off the oven and leave your
work to cool.

VARIATION

*Ceramic tiles can be
successfully stencilled to
create interesting and
unusual decorative effect.
The farm animals and
chequerboard designs
shown here would work
well in a nursery.*

STORM
lamp

Although the principles of stencilling on glass are similar to those of working on ceramics the difference is that while ceramics are opaque, glass is translucent, which makes for interesting decisions as to how you are going to decorate it. The technique I have used here is worked onto a storm lamp intended to hold a lighted candle, which can make a dramatic addition to a dining table or to light a dark corner. Take care never to leave a lit candle unattended.

YOU WILL NEED

- white spirit
- a soft lint-free rag
- stencil (press-out supplied)
- cocktail sticks
- coloured cold-cure glass paints of your choice
- white tile
- stencil brushes, one for each colour
- cerne outliner in silver and/or gold
- cotton buds
- crystal thixotropic gel no. 045 gold iridescent
- round-ended kitchen knife or palette knife (I used a plastic disposable knife)

ONE

Make sure the item you are decorating is absolutely clean and free of smears; wash it first with warm soapy water if necessary. Degrease the surface with white spirit on a lint-free rag to help the paint to adhere. If you are decorating the storm lamp as illustrated here, you might find it easier to slip it over a kitchen roll holder so you can have both hands free. Using the star stencil, stencil over the surface of the glass. You will need to hold the stencil in place by hand as tape would mark the glass. With a clean cocktail stick, decant a few drops of coloured glass paint on to the tile, taking this up with your stencil brush, remove surplus paint and stencil the stars with a stippling motion. This paint dries very quickly.

TWO

Continue over the surface of the piece you are decorating, working out the balance of the design as you go. You can easily make alterations at this stage by wiping the paint off with a damp cloth. Continue until you are pleased with the way it looks, varying small and large stars. Practise with the silver and/or gold outliners, which come in a tube, on the white tile until you feel you can control the flow.

*This bowl looks
particularly good with
water inside it up to the
imagined water line with
lit coloured floating
candles on the surface of
the water. The base of the
piece has been painted
with two coats of
turquoise glass paint,
which heightens the effect
of the water.*

TECHNIQUES USED

❋ stencilling using glass paints
❋ using texturing gels
❋ using gold and silver
  outliners

THREE

With the outliner, outline all
the stars you have stencilled
in. Wipe away any errors gently
using a damp cotton bud so as
not to disturb the stencilling
underneath. Allow at least 10
minutes for this to dry.

FOUR

Squeeze a walnut-sized piece
of gold gel onto the tile. With
the round-ended kitchen knife
fill in the stars with the gel.
Do not smooth the surface as
the uneven finish of the gel
catches the light when it is
dry. Allow at least 24 hours
for the gel to dry. You can
then paint over the gel if you
wish to deepen a colour with
the glass paints.

TEXTILES

Stencilling is a very effective way of adding regular pattern to fabrics. Plain fabric such as calico, with its natural cream tones, can be greatly enhanced with colourful stencilled designs to make charming cushion covers, curtains, table cloths, tray cloths, bed covers and many items of clothing: the possibilities are endless.

It is especially satisfying to be able to follow through a theme by co-ordinating a design by repeating motifs on curtains, cushions etc.

Plain roller blinds can be made interesting with the addition of simple stencilled motifs. As every type of fabric reacts differently to paint, it is advisable to try out your ideas on a test piece first before working on the finished piece and make sure that all surfaces are clean before you start working. You can experiment with painting onto an old faded piece of velvet to produce something similar to the old therom designs mentioned earlier. As well as spray paints there are a number of fabric paints available which can be heat sealed with a hot iron. Read the manufacturer's instructions carefully before going ahead with the project. An alternative is to make your own fabric paint by mixing latex or acrylic paints with one of the water-based glaze mediums which are currently available, enabling you to create your own colours. This can also be heat sealed. This medium can also be mixed with bronze powders to give a rich and luxurious look to your work.

LEAF-PRINT
quilt
Project by Caroline Brown

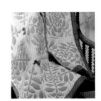

Quilting stencilled fabric is very effective and gives a delightful appliqué effect. The leaf shapes of this stencil are very easy to cut out, and the quilt squares have been stencilled in a random way, letting the colours gently overlap. The squares are individually quilted before being joined together.

YOU WILL NEED

- mask and goggles
- 40 x 45 cm (18 in) squares cream polycotton
- lining paper or newspaper
- repositional adhesive
- stencil (template page 128)
- spray paints in yellow, flame red, green, blue and brown
- 20 x 125 g (4 oz) pieces of batting
- pins, safety pins, cream quilting thread and needle
- beads (optional)
- 1 piece of polycotton sheeting for backing about 210 x 170 cm (84 x 68 in)
- 2 strips polycotton for binding the long edges, 220 x 15 cm (88 x 6 in)
- 2 strips polycotton for binding the short edges 170 x 15 cm (68 x 6 in)
- extra wadding for edges (optional)

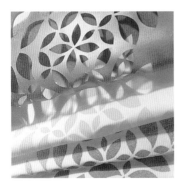

ONE
Wear a mask and goggles and work in a well-ventilated area. Lay a panel of the material on a flat surface covered with clean lining paper or newspaper. Apply the repositional adhesive to the reverse of the stencil and press firmly down onto the fabric. Lightly spray the stencil with yellow paint. Follow this with some red paint aimed at the centre of the design. This will give a glowing coral colour. To shade the edges use a little blue and green paint. Always hold a piece of folded paper in your other hand to help direct the spray. Remove the stencil and apply it to the next panel using more adhesive if necessary.

TWO
Lightly spray the centre of the stencil with blue paint then spray the edges of the design with a little yellow and red.

THREE
Make a sandwich of a stencilled panel, a piece of batting and a polycotton backing panel, with the batting in the middle.

TECHNIQUES
USED

* stencilling onto fabric
* using aerosol paints to
  achieve colour blends
* building a pattern from
  individual stencilled panels
* constructing a quilt

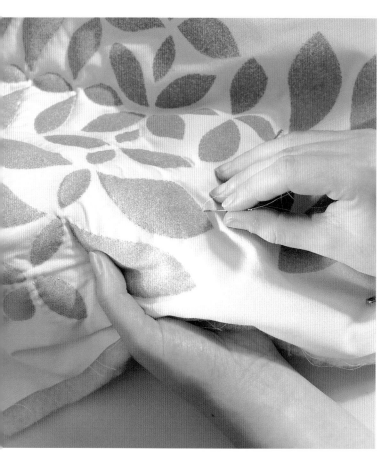

FIVE

Assemble the quilt panels in a harmonious pattern. Pin the seams together and machine stitch into four strips of five panels each. Trim the seams to 7 mm (⅓ in). Machine-stitch the strips together and trim the remaining seams. Press lightly on the right side.

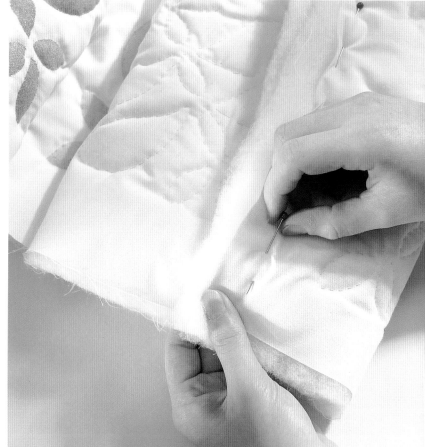

FOUR

Pin the layers together with safety pins placed about 10 cm (4 in) apart all over the design. Starting on one side quilt the layers together using a small back stitch or running stitch, making sure the stitches go right through to the back. (The quilting can also be machine-sewn.) Remove the safety pins as you work across the design. Sew on beads if required at this stage.

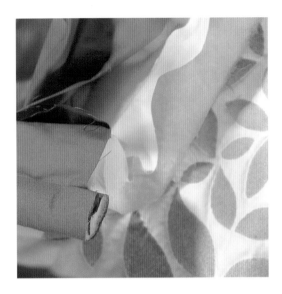

SIX

Lay the quilt on the piece of backing fabric. Knot the layers together in the centre of all the interior seams, working from the top. Bind the edges of the quilt with the strips of backing fabric, machine-stitched onto the reverse side of the quilt and folded onto the right side. If you wish to add an extra strip of batting, fold this into the binding before stitching down firmly by hand. Bind the two long sides first, then the two short sides, butting up at the corners. If desired you can also sew on small bows for extra effect.

CORNUCOPIA
picture
Project by Caroline Brown

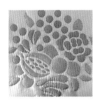

This stencil has been cut out in three parts. One for the greens, one for the reds and oranges and one for the blues. This is to keep the colours separate when using spray paints. On a small design it is easy to get too much overlap of colour, which results in a dull and muddy effect. For register marks, used to position the stencil accurately, I have cut out two leaves on each of the red and blue stencils. These are covered with masking tape once the stencil is in position.

YOU WILL NEED

- mask and goggles
- 2 x 45 cm (18 in) squares unbleached calico
- lining paper
- re-positional adhesive
- stencils (template page 129)
- spray paints in green, blue, yellow, flame red and a dark pinky red
- masking tape
- 1 x 45 cm (18 in) square 50 g (2 oz) batting
- safety pins, cream quilting thread and needle

ONE
Wear a mask and goggles and work in a well-ventilated area. Lay a piece of the material on a flat surface covered with clean paper. Apply re-positional adhesive to the reverse side of the leaf stencil. Press the stencil firmly down onto the fabric.

TWO
Spray lightly with green paint shaded with red. Remove the stencil. Remember to hold a piece of folded paper in your other hand as you are spraying, as this will help direct the paint.

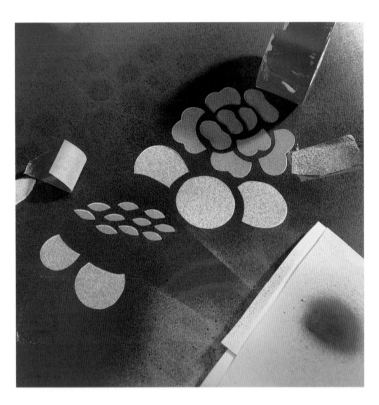

THREE

Use the leaf register marks as a guide to position the second stencil for the peaches and flowers. Once you have positioned the marks you should cover them with masking tape before you start to spray.

FOUR

Spray the peaches with yellow paint, shaded lightly with red. Spray red paint onto the flower and melon seeds. Remove the stencil.

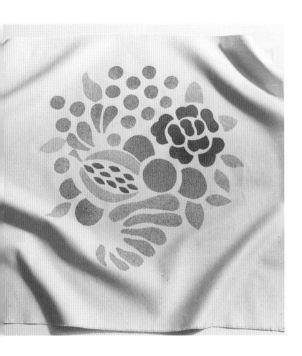

TECHNIQUES USED
* stencilling onto fabric; using aerosol paints to achieve colour blends
* using registration marks for accurate placing

FIVE

Again using the leaf register marks as a guide and remembering to cover them with masking tape, apply the blue stencil (grapes and figs) to the fabric. Using the blue and dark pinky red paint, spray the grapes and figs, adding more blue to the figs to make them darker. Remove stencil. Quilt the picture in the same way as shown on pages 62–63. To show the completed picture to good advantage, mount in a narrow, delicately coloured wooden frame.

CLAYFIELDS
cat cushion
Project by Caroline Brown

The Clayfields Cat appeared on the scene some years ago, a tiny starving scrap of fur. She has grown into a sweet-tempered beauty of subversive charm and winning ways. Her tabby markings were the inspiration for this stencil.

YOU WILL NEED

- mask and goggles
- 2 x 50 cm (20 in) squares unbleached calico
- lining paper
- re-positional adhesive
- stencil (template page 130)
- masking tape
- kitchen paper
- spray paints in yellow, red, blue, green and brown
- black waterproof pen
- cotton buds
- newspaper
- 1 x 50 cm (20 in) square batting
- 2 pieces 50 x 35 cm (20 x 14 in) calico for the back of the cushion
- pins, safety pins, red beads (optional)
- cream quilting thread and needle
- a piece of calico 5½ m x 12½ cm (6 yds x 5 in) for the frill
- cushion pad

ONE

Wear a mask and goggles and work in a well-ventilated area. Lay a 50 cm (20 in) square of fabric on a flat surface covered with clean paper. Apply re-positional adhesive to the reverse of the stencil and press the stencil firmly onto the panel of fabric. Using a strip of masking tape cover the cat's collar. Cover the cat part of the stencil with kitchen paper, stuck down with masking tape. Hold a piece of folded paper in your other hand to help direct the spray.

Spray the leaves green adding random touches of red and yellow to give a mellow colour. Remove the kitchen paper from the cat and mask off the leaves in the same way. Spray the cat with yellow paint, follow this with red and finish with brown to shade the ears, tail and back.
Remove the masking tape from the cat's collar and spray this blue or another colour of your choice. Mask round the collar before you spray.

TWO

Draw round the cat's features using the black waterproof pen to accentuate the eyes, nose, tongue and whiskers.

FOUR

For the frill, fold the long strip of material in half lengthways and pleat up neatly into a continuous frill. Machine-stitch 7 mm (⅓ in) from the edge and press.

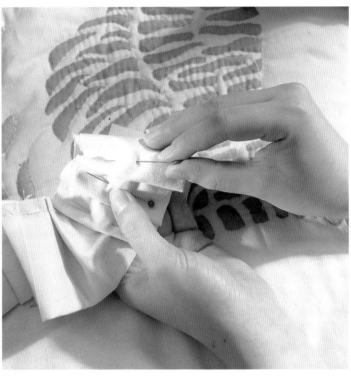

THREE

To add the red berries spray a little of the red paint into the aerosol cap, dip in a cotton bud and dot onto the fabric. Practise this on newspaper first, otherwise use a red waterproof pen. Quilt round the design as shown on pages 62–63, making a sandwich of the stencilled panel, batting and backing and stitch through all the layers. Sew the red beads on top of the berries.

FIVE

Attach the frill to the front of the stencilled cushion panel, raw edges together, with the frill pointing inwards. Machine-stitch in place. Where the ends of the frill meet, hand sew to make a neat join.

SIX

Make a 2.5 cm (1 in) hem along one long side of each piece of the two pieces of calico for the cushion back. Overlap the hemmed edges by 7.5 cm (3 in) to make an opening for the cushion pad. Machine-stitch in place. Lay the cushion back on top of the cushion front, right sides together. Pin in place and machine-stitch through all the layers. Trim the seams and turn cover to the right side. Iron the completed cover and insert the cushion pad.

MUSLIN
curtains

White muslin curtains with the light streaming through can not only be practical but beautiful. Stencilling gives you the freedom to decorate them in any way you wish, perhaps to pick out existing patterns already in the room where they are to be hung. Muslin also makes elegant bed drapes. The design can be stencilled all over or as a deep border with a narrow border as an edge, as demonstrated here. I love the effect of white on white, which gives an even more ethereal effect. I have used white fabric paint, which I have stencilled on with a mini roller. This is a quick and easy way of stencilling, provided the golden rule is maintained – use very little paint and build it up gradually.

YOU WILL NEED

- tape measure
- white cotton thread
- stainless steel pins
- scissors
- a length of muslin allowing at least 25 cm (10 in) to spare for hems, trimming, etc. and a spare piece for testing your design
- white fabric paint
- mini sponge roller and tray
- kitchen paper
- stencils (templates page 131)
- re-positional low tack adhesive

TECHNIQUES USED

❋ stencilling a curtain length
❋ using fabric paint
❋ stencilling with a mini roller

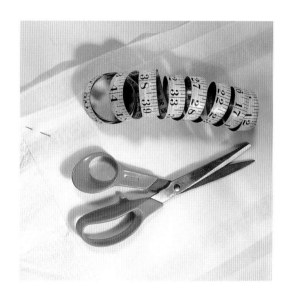

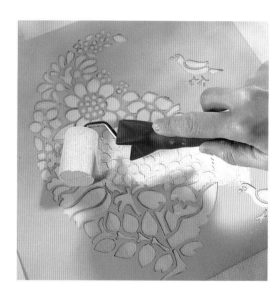

ONE

Wash and iron the fabric first to remove the dressing put onto new material by the manufacturers. Make up the curtain allowing a 7.5 cm (3 in) hem at the bottom and the heading you have decided on for the top. Iron out any creases in the material.

TWO

With a teaspoon, drop several spoonfuls of fabric paint into the well of the tray. Run the mini roller through this and work up and down the length of the tray to disperse the paint. Finally work the roller up and down onto kitchen paper until the paint comes out in a thin veil when tested. Test your design on a spare piece of fabric. Run the roller lightly to start with, increasing the pressure as you go; you will then find the paint does not come out too quickly.

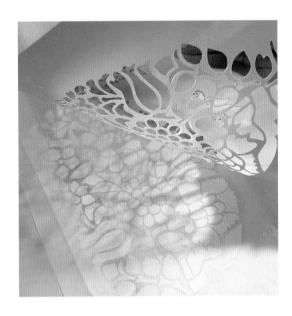

THREE

Pin the curtain onto the
ironing board, slipping the
kitchen paper underneath the
area you plan to stencil.
Having covered the back of
the stencil in re-positional low
tack adhesive, position the
stencil using the hem as a
guideline. If you are making
two curtains, position the
stencil so that there is a whole
pattern against the leading
edge of each curtain. If only
one curtain is to be made
start the stencilling at the
centre of the curtain and
work outwards towards each
edge. The pattern given for
this project has two little birds
on each side of the Paisley
motif, these can be used as
registration marks to make
sure the Paisley motif is always
evenly spaced.

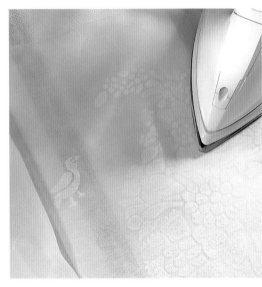

FOUR

When the stencilling is
complete and the paint has
dried turn the curtain over
and seal with a hot iron
according to the
manufacturer's instructions.
There is a second narrow
border given with this project
which can be stencilled under
the Paisley motif if required,
using the same procedure and
using the bottom of the
second stencil to make sure
that it is evenly spaced from
the edge.

SOFT *toy*

The stencil for the soft toy will either make a little doll which can hang at the end of a baby's crib or it can be appliquéd onto a bag, the front motif on one side and the back on the other. A child's name could also be stencilled on the bag. Use only textile paint which is non-toxic.

YOU WILL NEED

- pencil
- craft knife
- scissors
- stencils (templates page 132)
- paper doily
- masking tape
- 1 x 50 cm (20 in) length calico
- wooden board or ironing board for stretching the calico
- pins
- kitchen paper
- re-positional adhesive
- non-toxic textile paint in bright blue, bright red, white and black
- 3 stencil brushes
- white tile
- cotton bud
- iron-on interlining
- 1 x 2 cm (5 in) thick foam sheet – 25 cm (62 in) square
- tacking thread
- needle
- cream and black thread

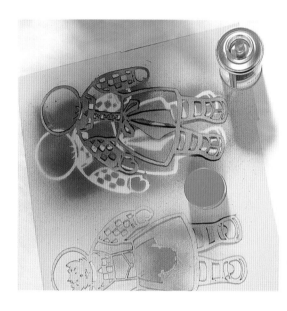

ONE

Wash and iron the calico first to remove any dressing. Trace stencil shapes and then draw a line around the whole stencil to create a narrow seam allowance around the edge. Carefully cut around this shape with a craft knife (before doing this refer to steps two and three). When you stencil, the paint will go over the edge of the doll shape and when this is lifted there will be a white line where the seam allowance is.

TWO

For an added decorative element you can add lace to the base of the apron by snipping off a small part of a paper doily.

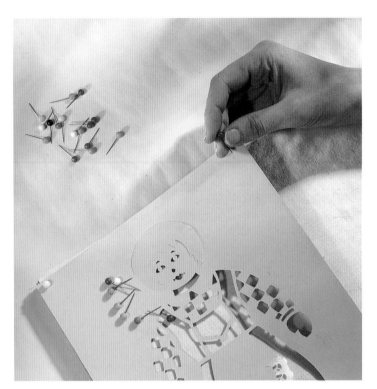

FOUR

Stretch the calico firmly across a wooden board and pin it in place. Place kitchen paper under the calico to soak up any excess paint. Run the re-positional adhesive on the reverse of both the front and back stencils and fix in place on the calico.

THREE

Attach the doily frill to the base of the apron on the front stencil with a narrow strip of masking tape on both sides. Do this after you have cut out the stencil shapes but before you cut round the whole shape for the seam allowance. Remember to keep the hair shape that has been cut out, as it will be needed later.

FIVE

Stencil in the hair and shoes in black on the front and back of the doll.

SIX

Leaving the stencil in position, stencil in the pinafore dress in blue, stippling firmly through the lace. Stencil in the blouse and striped stockings in bright red on the front and back.

SEVEN

To stencil the face, remove the stencil of the front of the doll and lay the hair shape in place. Mix a small amount of the red and white textile paints on the tile, adding the red to the white a little at a time until a flesh colour is produced. Stencil in the face with this, adding a tiny amount of red to colour the cheeks. Remove the mask for the hair, and replace the stencil. Stencil the mouth and the nose in red and the whites of the eyes in white. The eyebrows are in black. Stencil the flesh colour onto both of the hands, front and back. Remove the stencil and add the centre of the eyes with a cotton bud dipped in blue paint.

EIGHT

When the paint has dried, remove the calico from the board and iron on the back to heat seal. Cover the back with an iron-on interlining. Draw the doll shape onto the foam sheet, using the stencil if necessary and cut away the seam allowance around the foam shape. Cut the front and back sections of the doll on the seam allowance.

NINE

Tack the foam to the inside of the back section of the doll.

VARIATION

Although the instructions are for a doll with dark hair, different colours can be used but remember to change the colour of thread according to the colour of hair used. The stencil could be used round a child's room as a border and on a number of other items.

TEN

Take the front section of the doll and, carefully matching to the back, tack together making sure that the foam does not show. Using cream thread in the sewing machine stitch all around the doll with straight stitches 2.0 long. Turn the stitch length to 0 and the zigzag to 1.5 and zigzag all round the doll (apart from the hair) in the cream cotton. Zigzag across the base of the dress. Using a straight running stitch, stitch round the chin. Re-thread the machine with black cotton and zigzag around the hair as before. If you do not have a sewing machine, sew securely by hand.

FURNITURE

It is when decorating furniture that stencilling really comes into its own. Here you have the possibility to retrieve and transform unloved but useful pieces of furniture. You can also find furniture in junk shops, at auction sales or even by rescuing pieces that have been thrown away. It is, however, a good idea to look at the shape of the piece upon which you are about to spend some time and effort. If something is a really ungainly shape then all your efforts could be wasted.

Although suggestions have been given for painting furniture to be stencilled, very pleasing results can be achieved by working onto bare wood with the discreet addition of stencils in wood tones or folk designs in bright colours.

On the whole, provided the piece is in reasonable condition and depending on how much time you plan to spend on it, most items of furniture can be improved with a little thought and planning, and who knows, you may find yourself with a new decorative idea which is just right for that neglected piece of furniture which was so boring and unattractive that it had to be abandoned to the attic or cellar.

HANGING
wall cupboard

The panels have been used to demonstrate how effective a textured finish can be. Each facet is decorated with bright and cheerful ice-cream colours, finishing with a cone in the centre panel. To achieve a textured stencil a two-part stencil is used. The trellis panel of the ice-cream cone works particularly well with this technique. To achieve the ice-cream colours, use sample pots in strong colours such as shocking pink, lilac, pistachio green, all toned down with a lot of white.

YOU WILL NEED

- spray paint to make two-part stencil
- stencil (template page 133)
- low tack masking tape
- tube acrylic paints in cadmium red for the cherry, mid grey, yellow ochre, burnt umber, titanium white
- 3 stencil brushes
- white tile
- cotton buds
- non-permanent re-positional glue
- small disposable pot to mix the textured paint
- a tube of ready-mixed filler
- palette knife or flat-ended kitchen knife
- damp rag
- dead-flat acrylic varnish

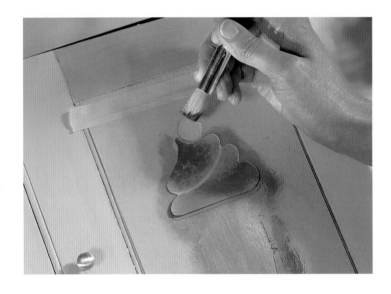

ONE

The first stencil consists of a trellis design, swirls of ice-cream and a cherry. Make a second stencil by laying the first stencil on a fresh piece of stencil card and spraying through the design with spray paint. Cut out the whole shapes – cherry, two pieces of ice cream and the cone without the detailed design and keep the shapes you have cut out for masking. Lay the second stencil shape onto the panel. Fix in position with low tack masking tape. To stencil the ice-cream, mask the cone with the cut-out cone section and stencil the ice-cream background in a mix of mid grey and titanium white acrylic paint. Remove the cone mask and, leaving the stencil in position, mask off the ice-cream section with the cut-out ice-cream section. Stencil the cone in a mixture of yellow ochre, burnt umber and titanium white. Stencil the cherry in red. With a cotton bud remove a highlight on the cherry while the paint is still wet. Remove the stencil and allow to dry.

TWO

Cover the back of the first stencil lightly with non-permanent re-positional glue. This is important because, to be effective, the texture mix must not seep under the stencil. Lay the stencil over the already stencilled basic shape to make sure it matches exactly. Cover the cone base with the mask as before. Mix together the filler, a little yellow ochre and titanium white in the plastic pot. Using the palette knife work the mix over the ice-cream section as shown.

TECHNIQUES
USED

❋ creating and using a two-
part stencil
❋ working with filler to give a
textured finish
❋ softening colours to give
vibrant or ice-cream
colours

THREE

Leaving the stencil in place, lightly mask off the section covered with the texture mixture. For the cone mix some yellow ochre, titanium white, a little burnt umber and some filler and work this over the cone area. Carefully remove the stencil and wipe it down immediately with a damp rag. When the filler has completely set varnish over the entire panel with dead-flat acrylic varnish.

LARGE
store cupboard

The cupboard used in this project was a wonderful find as it was destined for the skip. Once it had been stripped of its many layers of paint the quality of the wood and the care with which it had been put together became obvious. As it had many moulded panels on the front of the doors a design in Pennsylvania Dutch style seemed appropriate. I used traditional paints throughout because they give a mellow painted look to the work (although latex or emulsion paint could be used just as effectively). Traditional paint was also used for the stencilling. This paint dries very quickly, is easy to stencil with and can be bought in small sample pots, which are perfect for stencilling. It does, however, need to be sealed at each stage with acrylic varnish but both the paint and the varnish dry extremely quickly.

YOU WILL NEED

To prepare the cupboard:

- sandpaper
- sanding sealer
- wood filler
- 500 ml (16 fl oz) terracotta-coloured paint
- 3 x 5 cm (2 in) brush
- 1 household candle
- masking tape
- smaller amounts of pale yellow for the centre panel, and dark blue/green for the surround
- fine wire wool
- dead-flat acrylic varnish
- stencil (template page 134)

To stencil the designs:

- lining paper
- non-permanent re-positional glue
- 5 stencil brushes
- paint in deep yellow, deep red, charcoal, green, and white
- a white tile to use as a palette for the paint
- cotton buds
- kitchen paper
- clear wax
- soft cloth (an old T-shirt is ideal), cut into squares

ONE
Sand all over to provide a key for the paint. If the wood is new, seal with sanding sealer. Fill any holes or cracks with wood filler, and sand down. Paint the whole surface of the wood with terracotta paint and allow to dry. Using the candle, rub firmly over areas where there would have been wear – along corners, around any keyholes and occasionally in the centre of the panels.

TWO
Mask around the outside edge of the moulding with masking tape. Do this just before you begin to paint, as masking tape can be difficult to remove if left for 4 hours or longer.

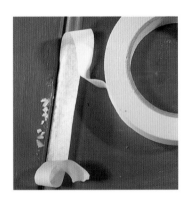

THREE
Paint the whole cupboard, except for the panels, with the dark blue/green paint.

SIX

Rub over the entire cupboard with fine wire wool paying special attention to the areas where the candle wax had been applied. The base colour will be revealed here and there. If you feel you have removed too much of the second colour, you can paint those areas again.

FIVE

When the tape is removed, the mouldings will be revealed in the terracotta base colour.

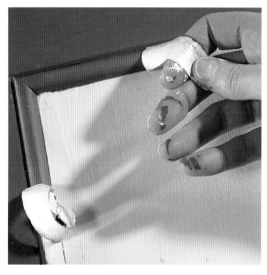

SEVEN

When you are satisfied with the way the cupboard looks apply one coat of dead-flat acrylic varnish all over. This will protect your work when you come to stencil and enable you to make corrections to the stencilling without the base coat being altered.

FOUR

Remove the masking tape and re-apply around the inside of the moulding and paint the panels pale yellow.

EIGHT
This cupboard has different-sized panels so the stencil is repeated vertically for the larger motifs. Try this out on lining paper first. Position the stencil on the baseline and slide it up to fill the large empty space. If you feel daunted by the idea of stencilling on all those little black dots, just leave them out – they can be put on later.

TEN
Cover the back of the stencil with non-permanent re-positional glue. First paint the tulips in yellow and, leaving the stencil in place throughout, paint the tips and bases of the tulips in red together with the pot.

ELEVEN

Stencil all the stems and dots (unless you intend to add them later) and little birds in black together with the outer parts of the pot. Stencil in the leaves in green and go over the birds in white. Remove the stencil. Now paint in the black dots for the eyes of the birds and the dots around the design if you prefer this method to stencilling. Use a cotton bud dipped in black paint with the surplus wiped off on kitchen paper. When your work is quite dry you can rub over some of the stencilling with fine wire wool to give a worn appearance. Paint on a coat of dead-flat acrylic varnish to protect your work. Allow this to dry, and then to give it a mellow, aged look use a coat of good-quality clear wax, rub in well and allow to dry. Finally, buff with a soft cloth.

TECHNIQUES USED

❋ rubbing back and distressing the base coat

❋ using a wax resist

❋ how to simplify the problem of having to pick out the mouldings by using masking tape

❋ using traditional paints to give a period look

❋ using wax to give a patina – this works especially well with water-based paints which seem to soak up the wax so that it becomes part of the final coat of paint in spite of the layer of varnish

COFFEE
table

This small low table with a drawer at the side did not look very interesting at first; the shape was chunky and not at all elegant. It was intended for a sitting room and by adding a chequerboard it could fulfil two purposes – a games table as well as a coffee table. Having painted it black to look more formal, it immediately seemed less chunky and rustic in appearance and much more suitable for the room for which it was intended. Black on its own can seem very stark and flat so by painting on a layer of barn red underneath and lightly rubbing away the top layers at the corners to reveal the red, the whole piece becomes warmer and livelier. The Turkish design and the gold lining down the legs and round the edges adds interest and makes the table more suitable for formal use.

YOU WILL NEED

- sandpaper
- wood filler
- barn red emulsion or traditional paint
- 2 x 5 cm (2 in) brushes
- high-gloss floor-quality acrylic varnish
- heavy-duty acrylic varnish
- black emulsion or traditional paint
- fine wire wool
- dead-flat acrylic varnish
- metal ruler (non-slip)
- a piece of white chalk
- stencils (templates pages 135–36)
- set square to ensure the corners of the chequerboard are square
- low tack masking tape
- red gold varnish
- kitchen paper
- pewter-coloured varnish
- white spirit
- permanent gold marker pen
- small marine sponge
- red undercoat paint
- small bowl or saucer for the paint to be used in sponging

ONE
First prepare the table for painting. Rub down well with sandpaper to give a key for the new paint. Fill cracks and holes with wood filler. Paint over the whole table in barn red paint. Allow to dry. Seal with a coat of heavy-duty acrylic varnish. Allow to dry. Paint over a coat of the black paint. When this has dried, using fine wire wool gently rub the corners and edges so the red base coat can just be seen. Varnish. Allow to dry.

TWO
Find the centre of the table by marking the centre of each side and drawing across to the opposite side with the white chalk. Where the two lines cross is the centre.

THREE
The chequerboard stencil allows for a board of 36 x 36 cm (24 x 24 in) square. Mark this out with chalk using a set square to mark out the corners as shown.

❁ sponging through a stencil

❁ using a gold pen to make
   lines

❁ measuring out a
   chequerboard

❁ using gold varnishes

❁ creating a lacquer look

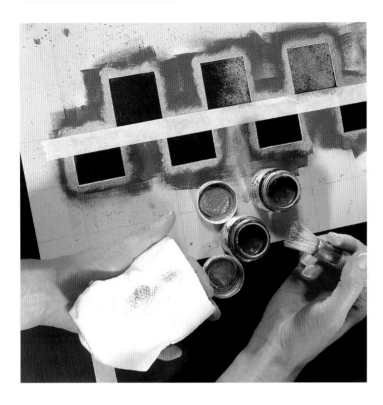

FIVE

Lay the stencil in position and
run low tack masking tape
over the far edge of the
squares on the second row.
This will keep the edges crisp.

FOUR

Stick low tack masking tape
around the perimeter of the
chequerboard area.

SIX

Shake the bottle of red gold
varnish well. You will find
when you open the bottle that
there is enough varnish left in
the lid of the container to use
for the stencilling. Take up the
varnish from the lid onto a
clean stencil brush and wipe
off the excess onto the
kitchen paper. Using a dabbing
motion so that the effect is
slightly transparent, stencil the
first row of squares. Remove
the low tack masking tape and
tape across the far end of the
first row. Stencil the second
row in the same way.
Continue across the board
until you have finished
stencilling all the red gold
squares. Then, reversing the
stencil, work all the pewter
squares in the same way.
Errors can be removed with
white spirit.

SEVEN

Lift off the stencil and remove the masking tape. Using the gold pen and metal ruler draw a line around the edge of the board. Also draw lines across the chequerboard in each direction. Again, errors can be removed with white spirit.

EIGHT

Position the stencil intended for each end of the table, laying the centre of the stencil on the chalk mark made to show the centre of the table. Wet the marine sponge then squeeze out as much water as you can so that it is just damp. Dip the sponge into a bowl containing the red undercoat paint and gently sponge this across the stencil.

NINE

Leaving the stencil in place, sponge some of the red gold varnish across the pattern.

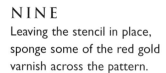

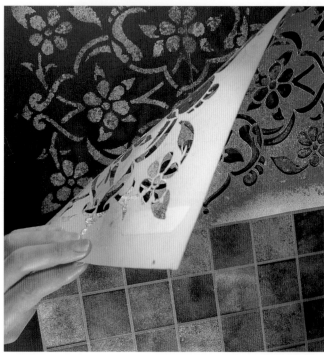

TEN

Stencil the other end of the table in the same way.

VARIATION

*A fruit-bowl design
in gold varnish would
also look effective on
the table.*

ELEVEN

Follow the same procedure to stencil the pattern down each of the long sides, matching registration marks as you work down the sides. Using the gold marker fill in the centres of the flowers, then draw a line around the edge of the top of the table. Turn the table onto its side and draw the lines round the edges of the legs using the metal rule. The pen's ink flows much better if you use it on an upright surface. Finally apply at least three coats of high-gloss, heavy-duty acrylic varnish. Allow each coat 2 hours to dry. If you prefer, you could stencil only one colour on the chequerboard, leaving the background as the second colour. This is less labour-intensive.

CHEST
of drawers

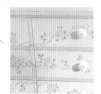

This piece was already a pretty shape and I was fortunate in that it was made of medium density fibreboard which had already been sprayed in white. This made an excellent base for a paint finish and I did not have to do any preparation work at all except wipe it down with a damp cloth and a little detergent to degrease it. This is the only project in the book for which I used artist's oil paints. These are quite suitable for stencilling but they take a long time to dry and therefore need the addition of dryers. The same applies for alkyd paints. If you plan to turn the stencils over to obtain a mirror image as I have done here then you need two stencils, one facing the other, as the oil paint will not have dried and would leave paint marks on your work when you turn it over. You need to leave your finished work at least several days to dry before varnishing with oil-based varnish.

YOU WILL NEED

- mid-yellow emulsion paint
- water-based glaze
- brush to apply the glaze
- tissue paper
- acrylic dead-flat varnish
- bright yellow, green/blue, raw umber, white oil paint
- white tile
- disposable plastic knife
- dryers (to speed up drying time of the oil paints; available from good art shops)
- white spirit
- brush for mixing
- stencils (press-outs provided)
- 3 stencil brushes
- lining paper
- kitchen paper
- disposable gloves
- polyurethane varnish
- lint-free rag

ONE
Label the position of the drawers with a marker inside so you know the order in which to put them back. Remove the drawers and, if possible, also the handles. The paint finish on this chest is frottage, so a glaze of half mid-yellow emulsion paint and half water-based glaze is used. Paint the glaze over the chest in sections, start with the top.

TWO
Lay crumpled tissue paper over the glaze and press down gently, then pull it away.

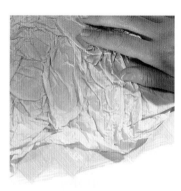

THREE
It leaves a soft marking as a base for the stencilling. Each section should be left to dry before going on to the next. When the glaze has dried paint a coat of acrylic dead-flat varnish over the whole chest, carcass and drawers.

FIVE

Having mixed your colours, test out your design on a piece of lining paper. Very little oil colour is needed and the stencil brush should be well worked into the kitchen paper to remove any surplus paint before you start. Never at any stage of the work put your brush into the white spirit, as it will thin the paint so much that it will run under the stencils. Use two of each rose and flower stencils if you plan to reverse them.

FOUR

Decant the paints onto the tile using a disposable plastic knife for each colour. Add a small amount of dryers to the tile. If necessary, thin paints a little with a few drops of white spirit. Mix the colour of the bows and ribbons, adding the blue to the white and gradually adding a little of the yellow and then the raw umber to soften. Stencil the flowers in yellow, with white added, and the leaves in green with yellow added.

SIX

First stencil the whole shape with a thin film of colour and then go over the areas like the centre of the bow, the ends of the bows, and the ends of the flowers for a second time to deepen the colours in these areas. Replace the drawers.

SEVEN

Stencil the rose and ribbon design around the edge of the top of the chest and fill the centre with the trellis design (template page 127). It is possible to see the shapes of the border through the trellis design and the stencils stop before overlapping the border. Stencil the bows on the drawers, just above the mark made where the handle was removed. The rose and ribbon design is made up by moving the stencils around to form a swag shape. Work out the combination on lining paper first. Reverse the design on the bottom drawer so that the bow comes under the handle, giving more balance to the design. Work the centre of the rose stencil onto each handle. Leave the oil paint to dry for several days, then using the original glaze, define the mouldings and area around the drawers by painting on two more coats of glaze, allowing drying time in between. Finally, apply two coats of polyurethane varnish, allowing drying time in between each coat, by the following method. Using protective gloves and a lint-free rag, dip the rag into the varnish and lightly wipe over the surface almost with a polishing motion. This avoids brush marks and gives a thin film, which dries quickly.

VARIATION

This project is a lengthy and time-consuming one. You may wish to omit some of the procedures, such as the frottage, or to use acrylic paints, that dry a lot more quickly, instead of oil paints. If you use acrylic paints, you would then use a water-based varnish as opposed to a polyurethane varnish. To simplify the project further, you could change the design, perhaps by omitting the trellis.

TOY BOX

This toy box was decorated for an 8-year-old boy. With its quaint soldiers standing guard, once again the source was the colourful designs of American folk artists and I hope these timeless designs will give him pleasure for some years to come.

I was also able to include a number of decorative techniques in this project. Although I have described all the processes used in detail, you may wish to make your box simpler, leaving out some of the motifs or even enlarging some of them and using fewer stencils. You may not wish to texture the leaves and flowers, and instead just stencil the soldiers round the base.

YOU WILL NEED

- white acrylic primer, enough to paint the box
- 2 x 5 cm (2 in) paintbrushes
- fine sandpaper
- sample pots of emulsion or latex paint in mid-yellow ochre, deep yellow ochre and bright red, 250 ml (8 fl oz)
- a fairly stiff old brush, 7.5 cm (3 in) wide
- dead-flat acrylic varnish
- flexible tape (useful to follow curves)
- acrylic scumble glaze
- easy mask painter's tape 6 cm (2½ in)
- low tack masking tape
- white tile
- 4 stencil brushes
- kitchen paper
- stencils (templates page 137–38)
- re-positional adhesive
- acrylic paints in deep green, ultramarine blue, titanium white, burnt sienna
- wire mesh (I have used a commercially produced copper texture sheet)
- paper doily or suitable length of lace for the tree stencil on top
- spray paint in deep red
- fine artist's brush for the unicorns' eyes
- floor quality, water-based acrylic varnish

ONE

This box was made from medium density fibreboard so the surfaces were already smooth. Remove the lid and retain the hinges and screws in a marked tin. Paint the whole of the outside with 2 coats of acrylic primer and rub down. To provide an interesting background for the stencils drag the lid and the whole box in mid-yellow ochre – mixing half-acrylic scumble glaze to half mid-yellow ochre paint. Paint the whole lid with the mixture. Taking the old stiff brush, brush firmly across the lid from side to side and you will find this leaves thin stripes of paint.

TWO

Set the lid aside to dry and repeat the process with the base, taking a side at a time. Allow to dry, and then paint over a coat of dead-flat acrylic varnish to protect the surface ready for stencilling. Run a line of easy mask painter's tape around the top and base of the box. Place a line of low-tack masking tape along the inside of the easy mask painters tape and then remove the painter's tape. This will create the area for the border. Using the undiluted mid-yellow latex, paint the area for the border. Allow the paint to dry.

FOUR
To create another thin border fix two strips of tape with a narrow space between them inside the outer decorative border.

THREE
Put a teaspoon of deep yellow ochre paint onto the white tile, dip a stencil brush into this and work off the excess onto the kitchen paper. Having fixed the border stencil in place with low tack tape, stencil working your way around the border you have painted. Mitre the corners as shown in the section on cornering (see page 25). When dry, seal the borders with a coat of dead-flat acrylic varnish.

FIVE
Paint the space between the two pieces of tape red. If you have any mouldings on your box they could be picked out in bright blue.

SEVEN

Stencil in the flower shapes
using bright red.

SIX

To stencil the lid, position the
tree of life stencil in the centre
of the lid using the re-
positional adhesive on the
back and low tack masking
tape to keep it in place. Stencil
the trunk first. Squeeze the
burnt sienna and ultramarine
blue onto the tile to make a
dark brown mix. Stencil in the
trunk and branches. Use a
mask to stop the paint
colouring the leaves and
flowers.

EIGHT

Slip the mesh texturing sheet under the stencil; with the dark green paint use the brush in a stippling motion to stipple through the leaf stencils, remembering to use a guard to prevent the paint from going onto the flowers.

NINE

To add texture to the flowers, find a suitable length of lace or paper doily (you will need as many pieces as there are flowers), using the low tack masking tape, lightly tape these behind the flowers. Refix the stencil over the already stencilled tree, mask out the leaves and trunk, spray through all the flower shapes (see page 26 for instructions on how to stencil with spray paints). Fix the soldier stencil in position beside the tree making a mark on the stencil to ensure that when it is reversed to stencil the other side, it is in the same position. Stencil all the red areas, the rosette in the centre of the hat, the trousers and cuffs. Leaving the stencil in place and using a clean stencil brush, stencil the coat in ultramarine blue. Finally with another clean brush using the burnt sienna/ultramarine blue mix, stencil the face, the stockings and the shoes. Add a little more burnt sienna to your stencil brush for the musket. Stencil over the stockings in white. Position the small birds on each side of the tree. Stencil initially in the burnt sienna/ultramarine blue mix, then with white paint.

TEN

Stencil the base of the box. Place the drum in the centre of the front. The stencil for this is in two parts. First stencil the whole shape in the deep yellow ochre. Place the second shape over the yellow base and stipple in ultramarine blue (note that this is a negative stencil in which the background is cut away leaving the design so that when you stencil, the first colour you painted will show the design). Arrange the unicorns on each side of the drum. Place the first unicorn in position. With the white paint stencil over the whole shape except the collar. Stencil the collar in red and the horn in yellow. With the burn sienna/ultramarine blue mix, add a little white and define the shape of the unicorn by stippling round the shape. Remove the stencil and add in the eyes and fill in the design on the collar with yellow. Reverse the stencil for the other side of the drum and follow the same procedure. Fill in the leaves around the drum using the texture stencil under the leaves. Stencil in the soldiers as already described. Reverse the blue and red coats of the soldiers on the front. Stencil a line of 3 soldiers along the side-ends of the box. To make sure that the soldiers are all the same distance from each other make a registration by cutting out a second musket behind the soldier so if you place the gun over the one on the previous stencil they will always be lined up. Screw the lid back into place. Varnish all decorated surfaces with floor quality varnish, at least three coats.

VARIATION

As a finishing touch you could complete the box by painting the inside of the lid bright red and stencilling the child's initials in the centre. This should be done before you screw the lid back into place.

FLOORS & FLOOR CLOTHS

Mats or floor cloths made of painted and stencilled canvas were first recorded in Britain in the 1720s and there are mentions of them being used in colonial America shortly afterwards. Covered with many coats of paint and varnish, they were a decorative substitute for expensive rugs from the Orient. Sadly, few have survived because as they became worn, thrift prevailed and they were cut down to cover increasingly smaller areas, some eventually finding homes as book covers. They can be glimpsed as a background to many of the charming eighteenth- and nineteenth-century primitive portrait paintings in early America. Also, with modern decorating materials the problems of surface cracking is reduced. With the arrival of linoleum, floor cloths were used less and less. Today there is a revival of interest in these mats and reproduced examples are often found in historic houses.

They are also enjoying a revival in the home because they are hard-wearing, needing only an occasional extra coat of varnish.

The earliest mats were typically decorated with a chequerboard pattern. Later, designs following the patterns of Turkish carpets were used. In creating a painted floor cloth you have ample scope to give full rein to your imagination.

PAINTED
floor cloth

The design that I have used for this project was inspired by an advertisement for a beautiful wool rug in the Mogul style and although the pattern is not as intricate as the original, being formed of only three stencils and a border, it has translated well to the flat canvas.

Floor cloths such as this are best laid onto a hard floor e.g. wood, quarry tiles or vinyl. If the floor is at all ridged several layers of newspaper can be used to act as a lining. As a safety measure fix into position with two-sided carpet tape or poster tack. Clean with a soft cloth or detergent but do not scour or scrub.

YOU WILL NEED

For the canvas:

- a piece of heavy-duty canvas 10 cm (4 in) larger all round than the finished size
- stapler/tack
- acrylic-based wood primer in white
- 5 cm (2 in) decorator's brush or paint roller for the primer
- sandpaper
- craft knife
- scissors
- set square
- PVA adhesive
- spoon

To decorate the cloth:

- latex or emulsion paint in deep red, ultramarine blue and yellow ochre
- 3 x 5 cm (2 in) brush
- 3 clean kitchen cloths or old T-shirts cut into large squares
- 2.5 cm (1 in) masking tape
- low tack masking tape
- stencils (templates page 139)
- acrylic paint in burnt sienna, ultramarine blue, titanium white, crimson red and yellow ochre
- 4 stencil brushes
- white tile
- brush for mixing
- floor-quality acrylic varnish
- a brush or roller to apply varnish

ONE

Make sure your piece of canvas is large enough for the stencils you have chosen. Iron out any bad creases. Stretch the canvas to ensure a flat surface to paint on. Staple or tack round the edges making sure the cloth is taut. Cover with several coats of acrylic primer; allow to dry between coats. Lightly sand the last coat and remove any slubs with a craft knife. Remove the staples and trim the mat removing any uneven edges with the scissors. Check the corners with a set square. Make sure opposing sides are equal. Turn the canvas over onto its face, and turn over a hem of 2.5 cm (1 in) all round, mitring the corners. Stick down with PVA glue, rubbing with the back of a spoon to make the hem lie flat.

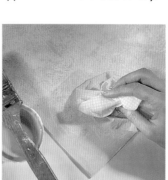

TWO

Paint over the whole surface of the mat with a mixture of half yellow ochre latex paint or emulsion, and half water. While the paint is still wet dab at the surface with a clean kitchen cloth until you have an evenly mottled appearance. Allow this to dry.

THREE

Using the 2.5 cm (1 in) masking tape, mask around the edge of the mat to the width of the planned border. Do this just before starting the next stage. Taking the second clean brush and kitchen rag, paint the centre of the mat using the deep red diluted with a little water. By painting the red over the yellow base a more interesting background can be built up rather than painting directly onto the white primer. Do not paint right up to the masking tape, or the paint may creep under it; instead use a dabbing motion with the kitchen cloth to bring the paint up to the masking tape. Again, dab over the surface with a kitchen cloth until evenly mottled. Allow to dry.

FOUR

Repeat the process around the area for the border using the third kitchen cloth and brush and using the ultramarine blue paint (diluted).

SIX

Using a clean brush, stencil the pale blue flowers with the ultramarine and white mixed on the white tile. Leaving the stencil in place mix yellow ochre and ultramarine blue to make green, and stencil the leaves with a clean brush. Deepen the tips of the flowers with a little blue.

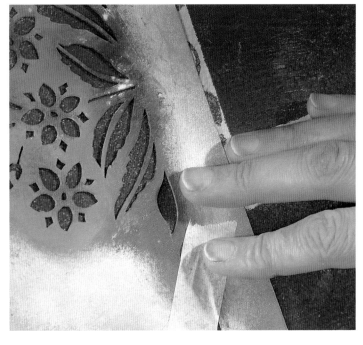

FIVE

Remove the masking tape around the border, and clean up any paint which may have crept under the tape. Decide which of the flower motifs is to be the corner piece for the border. Using low tack masking tape position the stencil in the first corner. Because the stencils are being worked on a rich background first stencil all the work with a light layer of titanium white. Do not remove the stencil. The white paint should dry quickly and will make the colours stencilled on top look far more luminous.

SEVEN

Stencil the flowers around the border in the same way. For the tulip-shaped flowers mix up a small amount of yellow ochre paint with crimson red and titanium white, and for the third group of flowers a little yellow ochre and titanium white. In each case deepen the tips of the flowers as you go along.

TECHNIQUES USED

❈ making a canvas floorcloth
❈ stretching canvas
❈ working out a border
pattern and creating
borders with masking tape

EIGHT

To work the yellow borders using the border stencil, work round just stencilling with burnt sienna. Because you are working on a pale background you do not need to underpaint the stencil in white first.

TEN

When the work has dried thoroughly coat with the floor-quality acrylic varnish. At least three coats of varnish are recommended. Allow two hours to dry. Allow four days for the varnish to cure before walking on the mat.

NINE

Register the border by placing the first flower over the last flower stencilled. Fill in the centre of the mat, working across each clump of flowers in rotation. As mentioned earlier you should have calculated how many stencils go into the mat when cutting the size of the canvas at the start. between coats.

DECORATED
floor

Decorated floors can be surprisingly hard-wearing and are an excellent substitute for a carpet or rug especially when stencilled across a wooden tongue-and-groove floor. There are many design options to choose from: wood stains can be used to give the effect of inlay parquet, a chequerboard design in alternating colours can enlarge a room and look particularly good in a hallway, marbled effects with classical borders can add grandeur or even a simple border running round a room can be effective. As long as the floor is in reasonably good condition the stencil design can be worked directly onto the floor. Stencilling provides an easy way of working a pattern across a large area.

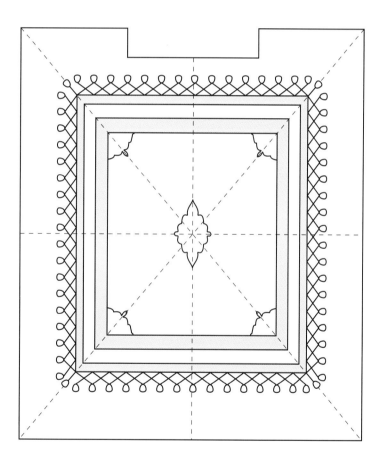

The design on the floor shown here was adapted from an antique Turkish rug, with richness built up by alternating broad and narrow borders. It is quite a time-consuming project as the design is so elaborate but the principles described remain the same even if you have something

simpler in mind. Most paints suitable for stencilling work for floors. It is the varnish that keeps the paint fresh and in good condition. Because the floor has been sanded and previous finishes removed the paint sinks into the wood adding to its wearing properties. It is a good idea to

store the stencils that have been used and to make a note of the paint colours so that minor repairs can be made over the years.

Before starting, a word of caution: when working on a hard floor such as this, always protect your knees by wearing knee pads or using a kneeling mat. If working in a totally undecorated room paint the walls first, so that the paint does not drip onto your sanded unprotected floor. Clear the room of all furniture. Having first checked that the floor is sound, pull out all loose nails or hammer these below the surface then sand down the floor. Industrial sanding machines can be hired by the day. It is a good idea to make sure that the stencils you plan to use are on a large enough scale and are not likely to be dwarfed by the size of the floor. Scale them up with the help of a photocopier.

To mark out the floor (Figure 1), you need to find the centre of the room and for this you need a chalk box. Ideally you need three people for this. The chalk box is filled

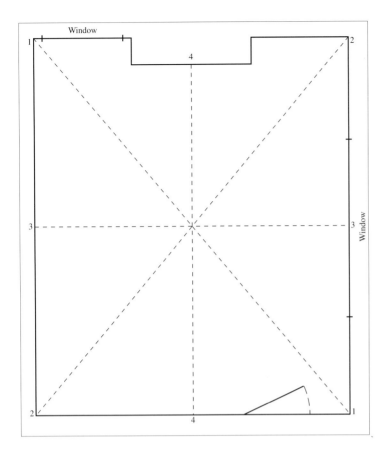

Figure 1

with chalk and contains a long length of string; as you pull the string out of the box it will be covered with the chalk. One person stands at each of two opposing diagonal corners of the room holding the chalk-covered string just above the ground. The third person stands in what is approximately the centre of the room, pulls the string upwards and 'pings' the string so that a mark is left by the chalk on the floor. Treat the opposing diagonals in the same way. Now make a mark at the centre point of each wall, and mark a line across the room from centre to centre of each side (Figure 2).

Now decide the overall size of the area you wish to decorate and mark this out with decorator's tape, using your chalk marks as a guide to make sure that the square is in the centre of the room.

Give the whole of the marked-out square a colour wash of half emulsion/latex and half water, wiping off the surplus paint as you go to give an even finish. This forms the background. Allow it to dry. The photograph shows the sequence of borders used. Mark out the borders using masking tape (you may decide to use fewer borders than shown here). Do not leave the masking tape on too long or it will become difficult to remove. Alternate broad and narrow borders.

Give the borders outlined by the masking tape a second wash, using other colours as background for the stencil. Also give the central motif and corner pieces a second wash as shown here if you wish, leaving the main body of the square with just the original

wash. When all the paint has dried, stencil first the borders then the central and corner areas. Mask over the central and corner motifs and stencil the all-over pattern across the main body of the square. When you have finished this remove all the tape. You can if you wish finish off with a tassel border around the whole square as was done here.

To protect your work use at least three coats of polyurethane matt varnish over the whole floor including the square, allowing at least 12 hours between coats. As maintenance, an occasional extra coat of varnish, perhaps once a year, may be necessary. To keep the floor clean, wipe over occasionally with a damp cloth.

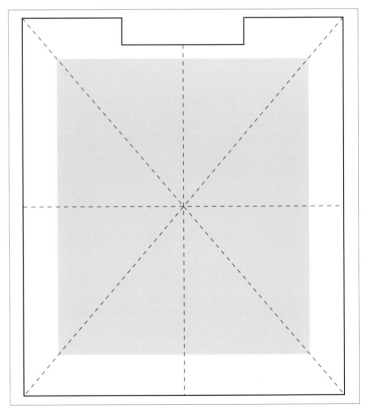

Figure 2

STENCILLED ROOM

Stencilling can be used to improve and enhance a room. Ceilings can appear to be brought lower by painting a band of the ceiling colour around the top of the room, reinforcing this with a stencilled border. A border can be stencilled at dado height, usually one metre (three feet) from the floor, breaking up a large space of a wall and altering the visual proportions of a room still further.

For rooms with a very low ceiling, bands of a running border can be stencilled vertically in stripes from ceiling to floor.

Decorating a room can be a large undertaking so take time over the planning stage. An advantage with stencilling is that the work can be undertaken in stages. Try to make your work easier if you can. Stencilling a border above head height can be tiring on the arms, for example, and it helps to cut a second long border with several repeats so that you do not have to position your stencils so often and work therefore progresses faster. It helps to assemble everything you need in advance. A shelf attached to the top of your step ladder to hold palette and stencilling equipment can save you running up and down. Protect the areas where you are not working with dust sheets and remove or cover any soft furnishings, which can be damaged with paints. A butcher's type apron with a large pocket in front to hold tape or chalk is helpful. Test the stencil colours against a sample board painted in the same colour as the walls.

BATHROOM

This room is a family bathroom used by children so I wanted it to look fresh and fun. In order to give the whole room this fresh feel careful consideration was given to the colours. The images to be stencilled were inspired by marine imagery. Although the end result looks quite complex, only four stencils and two stencil borders were used.

The side of the bath was marked out in panels using masking tape and sponged across the tape in the same colours as those that had been used for bathroom. This was varnished at the same time as the false tiles.

YOU WILL NEED

- 1 litre (1¾ pints) white latex/emulsion to match the ceiling and to paint the tiled area
- 4.5 litres (7½ pints) pale blue latex/emulsion
- 5 cm (2 in) easy mask decorators' tape
- Stencils (press-outs supplied)
- plumb line
- poster tack
- chalk
- ruler
- marine sponge
- sample pots of pale orange, pale lime green, mid-blue/green and terracotta paints, 250 ml (8 fl oz)
- 3 mini rollers and trays
- kitchen paper
- fine line masking tape
- 15 cm (6 in) ceramic tile
- 5 cm (2 in) roller and tray
- heavy-duty high-gloss acrylic varnish

ONE

In order to make the ceiling look lower than it is, a border of the white latex ceiling paint was painted around the room to a depth of 25 cm (10 in). The rest of the walls below this were painted in soft blue emulsion/latex, except for the area around the bath and behind the basin (where normally ceramic tiles would be placed) which was painted white. The skirting was painted blue to match the walls as were the architrave surrounding the doors and the panel along the side of the bath. Once the background paint had dried, a narrow border was stencilled just below where the white lowered ceiling and blue walls met. The colour for this was the darker blue/green.

TWO

A large diamond pattern was then stencilled over all the wall areas painted blue. First the white painted areas which were to have the tiled effect were protected with decorator's tape. Using a stencil cut out to the shape of two diamonds next to each other, this was positioned below the border, which had just been stencilled around the top of the room. A plumb line was used. The string was suspended through the two vertical points of the diamond down to the skirting, having fixed the piece of string at the top with poster tack. A second plumb line was suspended in the same way through the second diamond. The line shown by the two pieces of string was marked with a piece of chalk down to the skirting using a long ruler.

TECHNIQUES USED

❈ changing appearance of a room's proportions with paints and stencils
❈ stencilling using mini rollers
❈ marking out walls with a plumbline
❈ sponging through a stencil
❈ how to achieve a fake tile effect

THREE

The stencilling for this project is quick and easy. Dampen a marine sponge and squeeze out to remove all surplus moisture then dip into a saucer containing the lime green paint and sponge over the two diamond stencils. Move the stencil sideways and make a further two chalk marks in the same way, then sponge a diamond shape working all round the top of the room. The second row is quicker to do, as you only have to check your stencils against the chalk mark.

FOUR

Stencil the sea horses on every other blue space between the sponged diamonds. Put a few teaspoons of the pale orange emulsion/latex paint into a tray and run the mini roller through this. Run the roller several times across a pad of kitchen paper to remove excess paint. Having fixed the stencil in position, run the roller lightly across the design then, leaving the stencil in place, dip a clean stencil brush into the terracotta paint, remove the surplus onto kitchen paper, then stencil the edge of the sea horse to define the shape. Move the stencil across to the next blue diamond shape and continue the work. Stencil every other blue diamond until the row is complete. For the next row down, move the stencil across so the pattern of sea horses forms a diamond.

FIVE

To stencil the wave border around the area to be 'tiled', run a line of fine masking tape around the edge of the area painted white. Using the wave border stencil as a marker, run a second line of fine masking tape along the bottom of the border. Paint the area in between lime green. Leaving the fine tape in place, stencil the wave border in mid blue/green, mitring as the corner is turned.

SIX

To create the tile look, mark off 15 cm (6 in) squares using fine masking tape over all the area around the bath and behind the basin, having first protected the border just painted with decorator's tape. Use a 15 cm (6 in) ceramic tile as a guide. Then, using a second mini roller and tray with the blue paint used on the walls, run the roller over the entire tiled area including the fine line masking tape, which should be left in position.

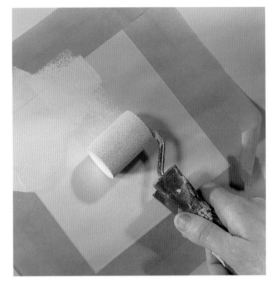

SEVEN

When the blue paint is dry mask every other square off with decorator's tape and, using a third roller and tray, paint over the squares that have been marked off with the lime green paint.

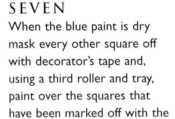

EIGHT

To stencil the fishes I used a pale orange emulsion and a mini roller. Place the stencil in position. Although there are only two fish stencils, I made these into a border as shown in the photograph using the tail of the first fish for registration, so that the pattern was always regularly repeated. Run the roller over all the fishes and then define the edges of all of the fish with a stencil brush and terracotta emulsion.

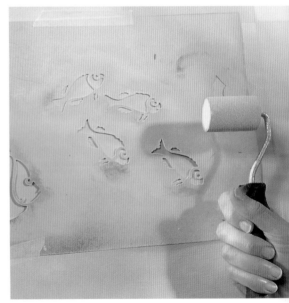

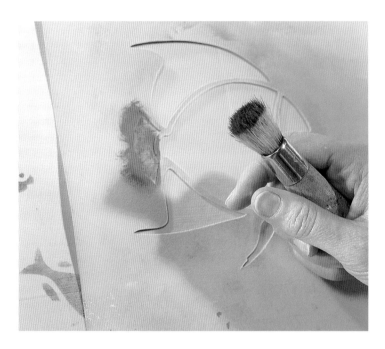

TEN
Stencil a co-ordinating border across the bottom of the curtain using fabric paints.

NINE
Move the stencil along using the tail as registration, as shown. When the stencilling is finished remove the fine line tape and carry out any touching up that may be necessary. With a 5 cm (2 in) roller and tray and high-gloss heavy-duty acrylic varnish, apply three coats of varnish over the whole of the tiled area allowing at least two hours' drying time between each coat.

INSPIRATIONS

◀ Mirror frame in a damask pattern with spray paint. The striped or dragged background gives the effect of an antique fabric.

▲ This dividing door was stencilled with sign-writer's paint. This paint is very suitable for glass – some varieties give a transparent effect similar to stained glass.

▲ Spray paints were used for this mirror surround, prettily decorated with blackberries and butterflies.

A Victorian pine corner cupboard with the old varnish removed, stencilled with spray paint onto bare pine and waxed afterwards with a good-quality wax.

This tablecloth was decorated with the stencil used for the lampshade, which forms a half circle. The stencil design was reversed to form a full circle.

This tray was stencilled with water-based wood stains which sink into wood to look like inlaid marquetry. The design can be outlined with a black permanent marker pen for further definition.

This tray was decorated with the stencil used for the jam pot covers, greatly enlarged. Acrylic paints were used. It was finished with a crackle-glaze in which a coat of water-based varnish was painted over an oil-based varnish. Because the water-based varnish dries quicker than the oil-based varnish it pulls apart as it dries leaving a cracked surface. Oil paint is rubbed into the cracks and when this has dried two coats of polyurethane varnish are painted over.

This stencil scene uses the technique shown in the bathroom project to create the effect of tiles. The radiator is decorated to match the floor-cloth shown below it and a radiator cover cut and sten-cilled to resemble pillars. The inspiration for this room design came from Portuguese tiles.

◀ Items stencilled with ceramic paint.

◀   This   bathroom   was
stencilled using spray paints on
a ragged background, using
imagery of doves, wisteria and
urns of flowers. The border
around the sink was repeated
with sand blasting onto glass
shower doors.

These photographs show part of the drawing room from a large Victorian hall. Stencilling was set to suit the style and size of the room. To give the suggestion of embroidery onto silk, the panels had a thin glaze dragged or striped sideways, after the stencilling was finished, across each panel to reinforce this impression.

TEMPLATES

Stencilling is about being able to create simple or complex patterns time and time again to great effect on a whole host of surfaces and items. In order that you can complete the projects given in this book and achieve professional results, templates for all of the stencils are supplied. Simply trace off, you can follow the instructions on pages 19–23 if you need a little help. If the stencil is not shown as an outline, a press-out is included.

The press-outs are perfect for the beginner who is perhaps a little cautious about cutting out their own stencils.

The designs chosen are extremely versatile and can be used in many different ways. All you have to do is give some thought to the effect that you want to achieve and think carefully about the arrangement of the stencils and consideration to the background on which they are to be used. Experiment and practice and once you have mastered the basic techniques, you can create interesting designs with professional results.

Lampshade

To trace at full size enlarge on a photocopier by 142%

Christmas Tablecloth

Garden Trug

Flower design for handle
included as press-out.

Tray

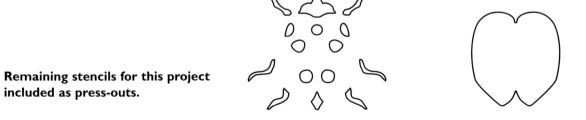

Remaining stencils for this project
included as press-outs.

Writing Slope

**Remaining stencils
for this project
included as press-outs**

To trace at full size enlarge on a photocopier by 125%

To trace at full size enlarge on a photocopier by 200%

Cornucopia Picture

To trace at full size enlarge on a photocopier by 142%

To trace at full size enlarge on a photocopier by 200%

Paisley motif/birds: to trace at full size enlarge on a photocopier by 178%

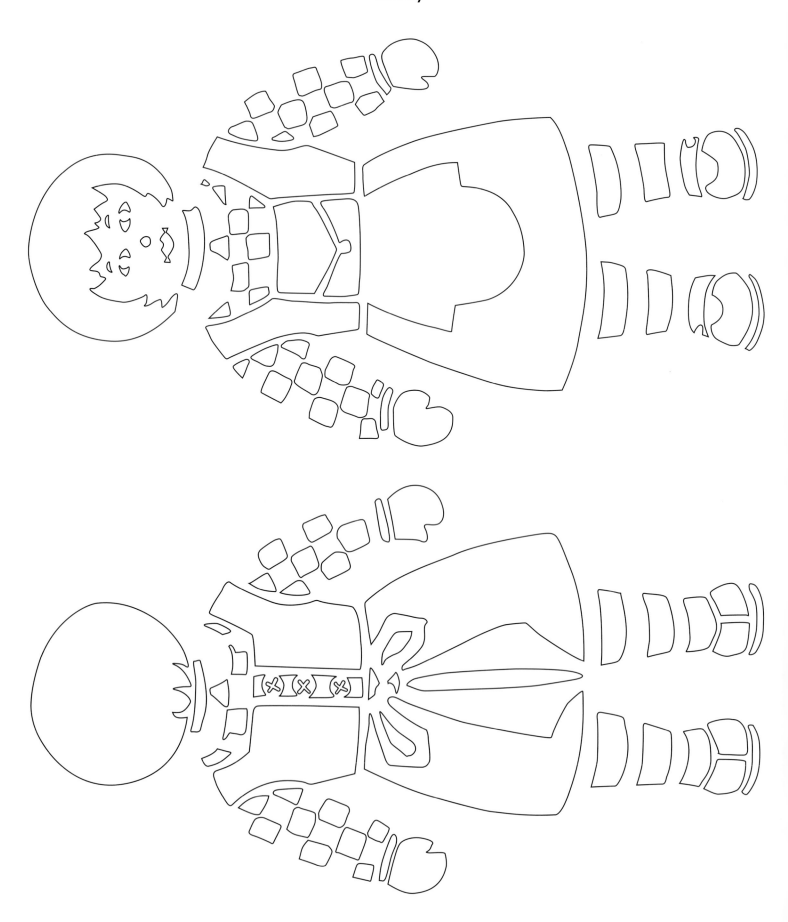

To trace at full size enlarge on a photocopier by 125%

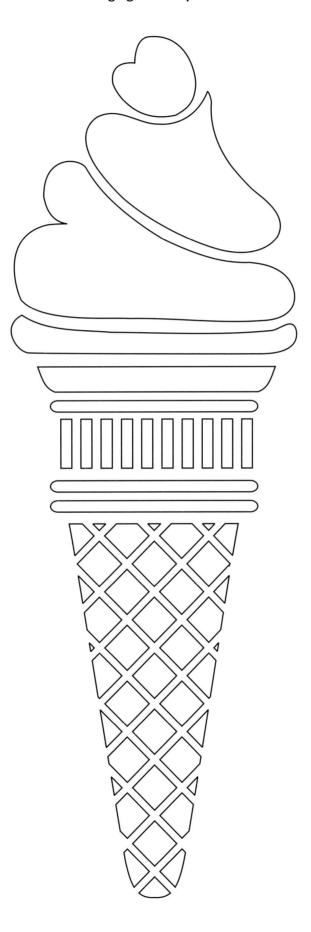

To trace at full size enlarge on a photocopier by 125%

**Coffee
Table**

**To trace
at full size
enlarge on a
photocopier
by 125%**

Coffee Table

**To trace at
full size
enlarge on
a photocopier
by 158%**

**To trace at
full size
enlarge on
a photocopier
by 170%**

Toy Box

To trace at full size enlarge on a photocopier by 277%

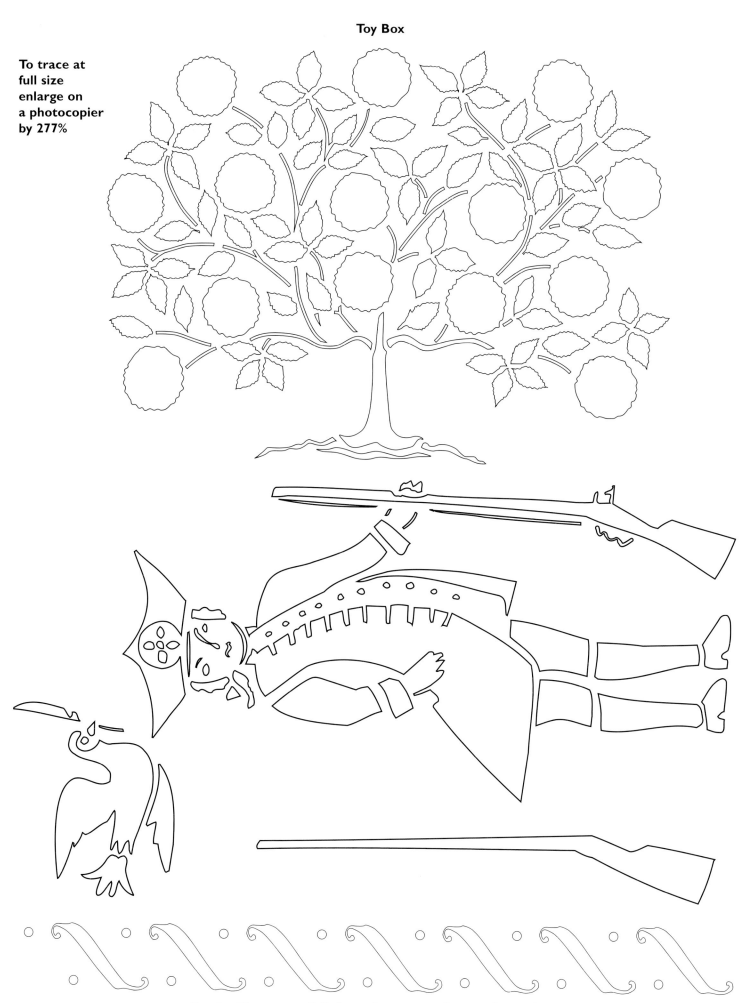

Border: To trace at full size enlarge on a photocopier by 220%

Toy Box

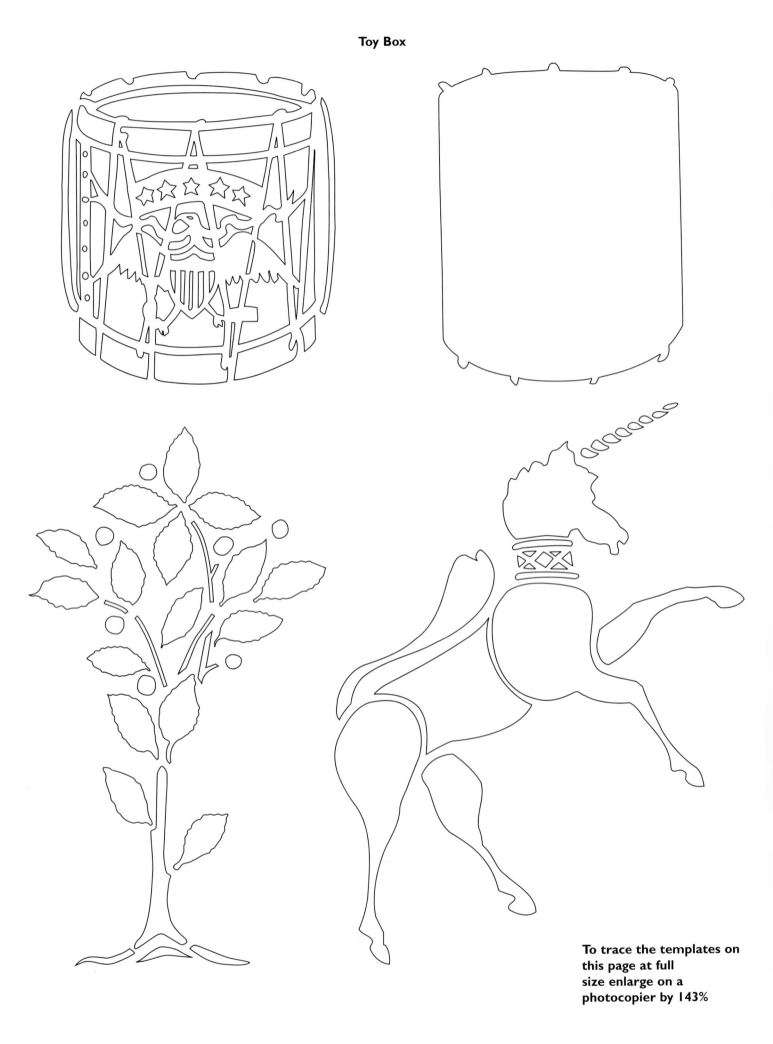

To trace the templates on
this page at full
size enlarge on a
photocopier by 143%

Painted Floor Cloth

SUPPLIERS

J. W. Bollom & Co. Ltd., J.T.
Keep & Sons Ltd.
P.O. Box 78
Croydon Road
Elmers End
Beckenham
Kent BR3 4BL
Paint manufacturers – contact
for list of suppliers. Keep's
Intenso signwriter's enamels
and superfine pigment in oil.

Brodie & Middleton
68 Drury Lane
London WC2 5SP
Tel: (44) 171 836 3289
Flame-retardant spray,
theatrical supplies.

Caroline Brown
Mount Pleasant
Lund, Great Driffield
N. Humberside YO25 9TP
Tel: (44) 1377 217729
Stencilled fabric panels for
quilting.

The Dover Bookshop
18 Earlham Street
London WC2H 9LP
Tel: (44) 171 836 2111
Large selection of books on
design; books available
containing copyright-free
stencil designs. Catalogue and
mail order available.

Fashion 'N Foil Magic
P.O. Box 3746
London N2 9DE

W. Habberley Meadows Ltd.
5 Saxon Way
Chelmsley Wood
Birmingham B37 5AY
Tel: (44) 121 770 6512
Artist's supplies, signwriter's
materials, decorative painting
supplies. Mail order available.

Liberon Waxes Ltd.
Mountfield Industrial Estate
Learoyd Road
New Romney
Kent
Contact for nearest stockist.

Philips & Tacey
Tel: (44) 1264 332171
Pebeo glass paints, ceramic and
fabric paints. Contact for
nearest stockists.

Pine Brush, Colourman
Coton Clanford
Stafford ST18 9PB
Tel: (44) 1785 282799
Water-based paints in
reproduction colours
(Traditional Paints).

P.S.W.
16 Alcester Road
Studley
Warwickshire B80 7NL
Tel: (44) 1527 853136
Graphic supplies, artist's
materials. Mail order available.

Relics of Witney
35 Bridge Street
Witney
Oxon OX8 6DA
Tel/Fax: (44) 1993 704611
Decorative painting materials,
Annie Sloan's Traditional Paints,
glazing mediums, pigments, etc.
Comprehensive mail order
catalogue.

Russell & Chapple Ltd.
23 Monmouth Street
Shaftesbury Avenue
London WC2H 9DE
Tel: (44) 171 836 7521
Canvas, artist's supplies,
'Golden' artist's colours
(acrylic). Theatrical supplies.

The Stencil Library
Stocksfield Hall
Stocksfield
Northumberland NE43 7TN
Tel: (44) 1661 844844
Large range of well designed
stencils and accessories. Mail
order.

George Weil & Sons
18 Hanson Street
London W1P 7DB
Stencil supplies, fabric paints.
Mail order available.

FURTHER READING

The Art of Decorative Stencilling;
Adele King Cile Lord, Viking Penguin 1976

The Art of Stencilling;
Lyn LeGrice, Viking Penguin 1986

Blue and Yellow Do Not Make Green;
Michael Wilcox, Collins 1987

Colour in Decoration;
Annie Sloan and Kate Gwynn, Frances Lincoln 1990

Decorative Antique Effects;
Annie Sloan, Collins & Brown 1988

Decorative Painted Furniture;
Maggie Philo, Meerhurst Fairfax 1996

Early American Stencils on Walls and Furniture;
Janet Waring, Dover Books 1968

The Flowering of American Folk Art;
Jean Lipman and Alic Winchester, Courage Books 1974

Folk Art Motifs of Pennsylvania;
Frances Lichten, Dover Books 1954

The New Paint Magic;
Jocasta Innes, Frances Lincoln 1992

Quilts & Coverlets & More Quilts & Coverlets;
Sheila Betterton, The American Museum 1982

The Stencilled House;
Lyn LeGrice, Dorling Kindersley 1988

Treasury of Turkish Designs;
Azade Akar, Dover Books 1988

ACKNOWLEDGEMENTS

I would like to express my gratitude to the following who have contributed to this book. First my husband for putting up with the mess, for his interest and a great deal of practical help. I would like to thank my son Simon for giving up time from a very busy life to put everything on his computer, and Jonita his wife for letting me loose on her bathroom. Their children Harriet and Nicholas have loaned me their furniture and Katy her ornaments. I would also like to thank my daughter Nell for lending her hands for the photographs and Penny, Jimmy and Harry for their support. Len Foxall kindly loaned his treasured period drum. Thanks to Gill and Bob, whose drawing room was shown, and Eric Grove for letting me use photographs of his bathroom. Many friends have offered help, especially Jim Snell who helped with the background information on decoration in old houses. Thank you to Nick Joyce, architect and historic buildings consultant of Worcester for giving me his time and the benefit of his knowledge on the restoration of historic stencil work and for loaning me samples. Thanks also to Mr Bill Hill of Hill & Co., Tadworth, Surrey, for allowing me to use the design inspired by one of his beautiful Oriental rugs. Finally a special thanks to Maggie Philo for getting me started.

I have greatly enjoyed working with the team from Quintet and would like to thank Clare for her patience and for her helpfulness and efficiency, Jonathan, for his painstaking and original approach to photographing the projects so beautifully, and Silke for her elegant styling.

The following people kindly gave or loaned equipment:
  J.W. Bollom & Co. (J.T. Keep & Sons Ltd) – superfine pigment in oil.
  Castle Nurseries, Studley, Worcestershire – weeping fig and other plants.
  Fashion 'N Foil Magic – heat pen.
  Liberon Waxes – gilt varnishes, wood stains and waxes.
  Phillips and Tacey – Pebeo glass paints and Porcelain 150.
  Russell & Chapple – samples of golden acrylic paints and pre-primed cotton canvas.

Picture credits
  Pg 8 Nick Joyce; pg 9 Reproduced by permission of the American Museum in Britain, Bath ©;
  pg117 *bottom* Lionel.

DIRECTORY

A

ACETATE transparent sheeting – a cellulose derivative. Can be used for making stencils and cut with a heated pen or craft knife.

ANTIQUING refers to various methods used to make a decorated object look older than it is. When done skilfully it can add a faded elegance to the piece.

B

BATTING wadding used in quilting.

BRIDGE strips separating the shapes within a stencil.

BRONZE POWDER powders manufactured in every shade of gold. Can be added to a medium such as P.V.A. to make a gold paint. Can darken or discolour but although not permanent, can give sparkle to a piece of work.

BRUSHES
Acrylic, artists' or nylon best for use with acrylic paints.
Decorators' brush used for painting in backgrounds.
Fine brush useful for adding detail.
Fitches flat brushes used in signwriting and decorating, sometimes with a chisel end. Helpful for accurate painting in awkward corners.
Stencil brushes come in various sizes and qualities; the bristles may vary in length and stiffness. Usually cut straight across the base.

C

CHALK BOX a device for marking out large areas e.g. a floor.

COLOURS primary colours form the base from which other colours can be mixed. They cannot be made by mixing. Colours used in the projects were:

Blue Monestial blue – an intense deep blue with greenish undertones. Prussian blue can be used in place of Monestial blue. Ultramarine – a brilliant blue originally made from lapis lazuli.

Red Alizarin crimson – a transparent dark red with blue undertones. Cadmium red – a permanent and clear bright red. Napthol crimson can be used in place of Alizarin.

Yellow Cadmium yellow – a bright warm yellow. Lemon yellow – a light greenish yellow.

Earth colours are formed from naturally coloured clays and earths. Those used were Burnt Umber, a dark reddish brown; Raw Umber, a cool greenish brown; Yellow Ochre, a soft warm yellow.

Neutral colours are neither too warm nor too cool and are mixed from a combination of other colours to form greys, beiges, stone etc.

Secondary colours can be made by mixing two primary colours together. These are: green, orange and mauve.

Titanium white is a permanent and dense white.

CRACKLEGLAZE or CRAQUELURE fine cracks across the surface of an object. Occurs naturally on some old paintings or can be artificially created as a decorative finish.

CURE the time taken for a material such as paint or varnish to dry to its maximum strength or hardness.

CUTTING MAT surface suitable for cutting on, such as self-healing mats, plate glass, hardboard.

D

DADO the lower part of an interior wall usually about 91 cm (36 in) from the floor which is marked off and decorated differently to the top half of the room. The rail which separates the two levels is known as the chair rail.

DAMASK in its true form, is silk woven in a reversible pattern. It also refers to white woven linen or cotton used for tablecloths and table napkins.

DEGREASING removing all surface grease from an object to be decorated to make it easier for the paint to adhere.

DISTRESSING a decorative technique in which the surface is deliberately damaged in order to give the appearance of age; a continuation of the process of antiquing.

DRAGGING or STRIPING a technique originally used in woodgraining, where a contrasting surface glaze is painted over the base coat and then a brush is pulled sideways through the glaze leaving a striped mark. Dragging can also be used to effect through a stencil plate.

DRESSING manufacturers add a dressing to fabrics when new to give them more body and added weight. If the fabric is to be painted this needs to be removed by washing, so that the paint can be absorbed into the fibres of the fabric.

E

EMBOSSED raised in relief.
ETCHED GLASS a design formed through the action of an acid. A similar effect can be achieved with special caustic paste painted through a stencil plate, or simulated with spray paints giving a frosted appearance.

F

FIRE-RETARDANT SPRAY for use on fabrics or surfaces that are exposed to heat, such as candle shades, electric light shades etc. Obtainable from shops dealing in theatrical supplies and DIY shops.

FLOORCLOTH early name for a floor mat. Usually made of heavy duty canvas which has been painted and varnished.

FOLK ART art, handicrafts and ornaments produced by people who are not technically trained artists but have grown up with the traditions passed from one generation to another. The work produced is usually fresh and sometimes naive, but frequently appealing. This type of art reveals the characteristics of the region in which it was painted.

FROTTAGE a paint finish in which the top glaze is textured by laying a sheet of crumpled paper over a contrasting glaze and pressed down to reveal the base colour in a random pattern when the paper is pulled away.

G

GRID METHOD OF ENLARGING a simple method for enlarging motifs. Used also for mural painting.

H

HALF DROP term used in pattern making. A single pattern in its entirety is called a repeat. If a pattern is to be used to cover a whole area such as a wall it is usually repeated regularly by working the pattern at equal intervals from top to bottom, making a single patterned stripe. The next row down can either be made to match exactly the preceding one or the pattern can be started halfway down the pattern on the preceding row. This is called a half drop repeat. The third row is the same as the first, and the fourth row the same as the second.

HEAT SEALING certain fabric paints can be made permanent and resistant to washing by sealing with a hot iron (on the reverse side of the painted fabric) at a temperature tested and recommended by the manufacturer.

HUE the description used to explain the actual colour of something, e.g. variations of green – a blue green or a yellowish green. Sometimes it is possible to describe a colour by referring to nature, e.g. sea green or leaf green.

I

IMAGE the likeness or representation of something. A mirror image is a likeness of a design in reverse, useful in pattern making.

K

KEY (in this context) to prepare a surface so that it can hold the paint. If the surface is very slick, e.g. a surface painted with gloss paint or a formica surface, it would need to be roughened with sandpaper in order for the paint to be able to grip.

KNOCKING BACK if a design is very bright and appears to 'jump' out of its background this can be irritating; this can be softened by gently dabbing a small amount of the background colour over the design making it appear to blend in with the background.

L

LEAD PAINT any paint marked as containing lead is not suitable for painting items to be used by children or surfaces that children will come into contact with.

LIMING WAX modern liming wax is made from wax containing white pigment. Traditionally used on oak where the white goes into the grain of the wood to give a pleasing speckled appearance; can be used on other woods.

LINING here used to describe the making of fine lines to set off a piece of work, such as on boxes and pieces of furniture. Traditionally a technique used by coach painters, this was an exacting craft requiring practise. However a number of short cuts have been shown throughout this book which can be effective to frame and enhance a piece of stencilled work which do not require a lot of practise.

LINOLEUM hardwearing flooring manufactured from linseed oil, resins and fillers.

LOW TACK TAPE the best sort of tape to use when stencilling as it does not pull away the surface onto which it is stuck.

M

MANILA CARD oiled with linseed oil, it is the card traditionally used for making stencils.

MARKER PENS available in a variety of colours. The point can be thick or thin and the ink permanent or non-permanent in which case the work needs to be sealed. Very useful for filling in detail and making lines.

MARQUETRY decoration using veneers of different types of wood. Used on furniture and panelling.

MATTE a dead flat surface appearance which does not reflect the light or shine.

MEDIUM DENSITY FIBREBOARD (M.D.F.) board made of particles of wood fibre and a binding agent. Much in favour for furniture making and small objects previously made of natural wood. Protective masks should be worn when cutting or sanding M.D.F.

MITERING a method of turning a corner when stencilling.

MOULDING an ornamental strip of wood which can be used as an edging e.g. around picture frames, as a dividing chair rail, on a wall, etc.

MYLAR a trade name for polyester plastic sheeting suitable for cutting stencils from.

N

NEGATIVE STENCIL the background of the stencil is cut away leaving the design uncut.

P

PAINT FINISH describes the various ways of distressing the surface of a painted area by covering the base coat with a wash, made up of either paint and water or paint and glaze, and while the wash is still wet, texturing or patterning the surface so that it comes away in areas to reveal the base coat.

PAINTS

Acrylic made by dispersing colour pigment in acrylic resins, water soluble.

Alkyd paints made from synthetic resins. Have many of the properties of oil paints but dry quicker because they contain a drying oil.

Binders the materials used to hold the paint pigment to the base medium.

Ceramic paints some are solvent based and fired at high temperatures to sink into the surface glaze. For stencilling, water soluble paints can be used, which can be cured in a domestic oven.

Emulsion or latex water soluble paints used frequently for home decoration and are suitable for stencilling. These paints dry quickly and sample pots are usually available from DIY shops.

Fabric paints suitable for decorating on fabric. Follow manufacturers instructions.

Glass paints water-soluble paints are available which cure to enamel hardness and are suitable for stencilling.

Japan paints pigment ground in oil free resin varnish. Very quick drying. Excellent for stencilling.

Non-toxic paints these should always be used when painting items or surfaces that children will come into contact with.

Oil paints can be used for stencilling although slow drying times can present problems.

Sign writers' paints similar in style to Japan paints, although not as fine.

Spray paints available in a wide variety of colours, can be used to great effect, particularly to achieve subtle colour blends.

Traditional paints give a chalky finish compatible with a period look.

PALETTE a surface such as a ceramic tile to hold the colours to be used in a project or a complete range of colours.

PAPER

Carbon used to make copies. Useful for transferring a design onto stencil card.

Cartridge the coarser grades of drawing paper.

Graph marked out with grid lines. Useful for designing.

Graphite thin paper coated on one side with graphite for transferring designs. Marks easily erasable.

Lining paper used in household decorating for underlining wallpaper. Is a cheap paper to use for sketching and testing designs.

Tracing transparent paper used to reproduce a design.

PENNSYLVANIA DUTCH folk designs of German origin (when used as descriptive design term).

PERIOD LOOK incorporates the design characteristics of a certain period or time in history.

PINKING SHEARS scissors with a serrated edge which can be used to stop material fraying or to give a decorated edge.

PLUMB LINE or BOB a length of string with a weight on the end to check on the straightness of a vertical line.

POSITIVE STENCIL the design is cut out from the stencil plate and paint passed through the holes created onto the surface to be decorated.

P.V.A. (POLYVINYL ACETATE) a clear, white synthetic resin used in glues and for mixing with bronze powders etc.

R

RAGGING a paint finish where a contrasting glaze is painted over a base coat and the glaze, while still wet, manipulated with a rag to leave random marking.

REGISTRATION MARK a mark cut onto a stencil plate which helps with repeating the design.

REPEATED BORDER a border made by repeating the same design regularly, using registration marks.

REPOSITIONAL ADHESIVE makes the back of the stencil tacky so that it will adhere to the surface to be decorated and prevent the paint creeping underneath.

RESIST painting certain areas with a material that paint will not adhere to, so that when the work is finished it can be sanded and the paint will come away in those areas. Used in *Antiquing* and *Distressing*.

ROLLERS made of foam, those useful for stencilling are the 5 cm (2 in) and 15 cm (6 in).

RUBBING BACK an antiquing technique where several layers of paint, often of different colours, are sanded down to show the layers of previous colours to simulate wear.

RUNNING BORDER a decorated border formed of a repeating pattern.

S

SAMPLE BOARD a board painted with the colours and design that are to be used for a piece of work. A useful reference.

SCUMBLE a thin layer of transparent medium containing pigment which can be used as a glaze over a base coat. Glazes can either be oil or acrylic based.

SET SQUARE geometric device used to check that a corner is square.

SOLVENT used to dissolve resins in certain paints and varnishes. Can be flammable and fumes can be noxious. Should be treated with care and manufacturers instructions should be followed.

SPIRIT LEVEL a measuring device to check that horizontal measurements are aligned.

SPONGING a paint finish using a marine sponge to make textural marks.

STAY WET PALETTE commercially produced to keep acrylic paints moist.

STENCIL drawing or printing plate with parts cut out to form a design that is copied onto a surface and paint applied over the cut-out parts.

STIPPLING a paint finish made by tapping or pouncing a stiff brush over a surface, giving the appearance of orange peel.

T

TAILORS' CHALK used for marking fabrics, can be dusted away after use.

TAPE

Decorators paper tape that is adhesive along one edge.

Fine line used by signwriters to mark very fine lines.

Low tack does not adhere too strongly, so is ideal to hold stencils in position.

Masking versatile, so is widely used in decorative painting.

Signwriters low tack tape available in various widths used by signwriters.

Stretch can be worked to go around curved surfaces.

Two sided used for securing carpets or mats to the floor.

TEMPLATE a pattern used as a guide for making designs.

TEXTURING imprinting a flat surface to give a raised or textured appearance.

THEROM STENCILLING stencil without bridges so that the work looks hand painted.

TIFFANY GLASS Art Nouveau period glass decorated with abstract patterns and organic forms in iridescent colours.

TONE the range of shades within a colour going from light to dark.

TOXIC a poisonous or harmful substance.

TRANSLUCENT allows light to shine through.

V

VARNISH transparent film painted over a finished piece of work that dries to a hard finish to protect it. Can be either gloss, satin, matte or dead flat which reflects no light at all. Can be either solvent based, removed with white spirit, or water-based containing acrylics. The higher the gloss the harder the finish.

W

WAX good quality furniture wax can be used for finishing. Dark stained wax can be used to give an antique appearance. Blobs of wax can also be used as a resist.

WHITE SPIRIT used as a paint thinner and a degreasing agent.

WOOD PRIMER used to prime bare wood so that subsequent coats of paint will adhere.

WOOD STAIN can be found in colours to simulate a large variety of woods and are now made with an acrylic water-solvent base.

Gift-wrap/Trug–handle

Christmas Tablecloth/Storm Lamp

Christmas Tablecloth

Tray/Ceramic Jug

Picture Frame

Bathroom

Bathroom